The Final Test

A Biography of

James Ball Naylor

Photo courtesy of the Morgan County Historical Society

The Final Test

A Biography of

James Ball Naylor

By

Theresa Marie Flaherty

www.TursasPublishing.com

No part of this publication may be reproduced or transmitted in any form or by any means, electronic or technical, including photocopying, recording, or by any information storage or retrieval system, without permission in writing from the publisher, except by a reviewer who may quote brief passages in a review.

Copyright © 2011 by Theresa Marie Flaherty
All Rights Reserved.

10 9 8 7 6 5 4 3 2 1

Photo credits (numbers refer to photograph sequence):
Courtesy of the Morgan County Historical Society, 1, 7, 28; Robert Wetherell, 2-3; Jean Naylor Finley, 4-5, 20-23, 44; D. W. Garber, 10, 33, 35; Lucile Naylor, 11, 45; Greg and Ellen Hill, 12, 18, 31, 36, 39, 40, 46; Norris F. Schneider, 13; James W. Mason, 14; The Morgan County Herald, 16, 17, 32, 42; Rick Shriver, 19, 27; Robert Naylor, 41, 43.

Cover Design by Michael Flaherty.
Cover image courtesy of Jean Naylor Finley.

Publisher's Cataloging-in-Publication
(Provided by Quality Books, Inc.)

Flaherty, Theresa Marie.
　　The final test : a biography of James Ball Naylor / by Theresa Marie Flaherty.
　　p. cm.
　　Includes bibliographical references and index.
　　ISBN-13: 978-0-9832342-4-1
　　ISBN-10: 0-9832342-4-8

　　1. Naylor, J. B.--(James Ball),--1860-1945.
2. Authors, American--Ohio--Biography. 3. Physicians--Ohio--Biography. 4. Politicians--Ohio--Biography.
I. Title.

PS3527.A92F53 2011　　　　813'.52
　　　　　　　　　　　　　QBI11-600020

www.TurasPublishing.com

For
Wesley

The Final Test

When all is said and all is done,
When all is lost or all is won—
In spite of musty theory,
Of purblind faith and vain conceit,
Of barren creed and sophistry:
In spite of all—success, defeat,
The Judge accords to worst and best,
Impartially, this final test:

What hast thou done with brawn and brain,
To help the world to lose or gain
An onward step? Canst reckon one
Unselfish, brave or noble deed,
That thou—nor counting cost! Hast done
To help a brother's crying need?
Not what *professed* nor what *believed*—
But *what good thing hast thou achieved!*

James Ball Naylor

Table of Contents

List of Illustrations		ix
Introduction		1
Chapter		
1	The Delectable Days of Childhood	5
2	What are you going to be?	18
3	S. Q. Lapius Emerges	29
4	Pleasures and Passions	40
5	Serialized and Historical Fiction	50
6	Success as a Novelist	59
7	Marketable Endeavors	70
8	Writing for a Younger Audience	85
9	Speaker and Entertainer	96
10	The Political Arena	116
11	Last Years	142
Notes		153
Acknowledgments		165
The Writings of James Ball Naylor		169
Bibliography		174
Index		177

List of Illustrations

Fig.	Description	Page
	Portrait of Naylor	ii
1.1	Robert W. Naylor	6
1.2	Naylor as a Child	6
1.3	Naylor Birthplace	7
1.4	Naylor Farm Buildings	7
1.5	Stockport Mill	10
1.6	Packet Boat at the Dock at Malta	15
2.1	Gatewood Portrait	21
2.2	Gatewood Drug Store	22
2.3	Naylor with Beard	23
2.4	Naylor's Wife Lena Ervilla	24
2.5	Naylor's Business Card	25
2.6	Naylor's Apartment over the Coulson store	27
3.1	Malta Railway Station	31
3.2	The Country Doctor	33
4.1	Malta Flood in 1898	42
4.2	Street in Early Malta	43
4.3	Elmhurst	44
4.4	Naylor's Office on Bell Street	45
4.5	Mrs. Naylor in 1913	46
4.6	Naylor Outdoors	47

List of Illustrations
Continued

Fig.	Description	Page
4.7	Naylor Family	48
5.1	Naylor with Harry Westerman	53
6.1	Stockport Street	59
6.2	*Ralph Marlowe* with Dust Jacket	65
6.3	Burroughs Book Store	67
7.1	Naylor's Office Upstairs	76
7.2	Naylor, the Author	79
7.3	Ad for Songs From the Heart of Things	83
8.1	Witch Crow and Barney Bylow	86
8.2	Naylor's Children	93
9.1	Muskingum Valley Chautauqua	97
9.2	Garber Poster	98
9.3	Naylor the Entertainer	101
9.4	Butler Entertainment Program	103
9.5	Naylor Admittance Ticket	105
9.6.	Naylor with Lucile and Olive	109
9.7	1908 Entertainment Program	110
9.8	Entertainment Brochure of Photos	113
10.1	Naylor for Senate	120
10.2	Glee Club Banquet	124
10.3	Malta Depot During WWI	133

List of Illustrations

Continued

Fig.	Description	Page
10.4	Naylor's Bookplate	141
11.1	Doty Twins	146
11.2	Receiving Marietta Honorary Degree	148
11.3	Naylor Family	149

JAMES BALL NAYLOR

Introduction

Without Dwight Wesley Garber, this book would not exist. Wesley, as I came to call him over the many years of our friendship, was a light in my life, and the driving force behind this biography.

Just over a hundred years ago in Butler, Ohio, as a young boy, Wesley was delighted to meet Dr. James Ball Naylor, who was then at the height of his popularity. Naylor was a friend of Wesley's father, J. S. Garber, and Wesley had read Naylor's novel, *Cabin in the Big Woods*. Later he read Naylor's other novels, and they became part of his growing collection of books and memorabilia about Naylor and Ohio. His life-long interest in the life of Naylor was launched.

Wesley, a sixth generation "Buckeye," became an accomplished Ohio historian, authoring numerous articles for the Ohio Historical Society and Ohio newspapers about people, places and events in Ohio history. He wrote *Waterwheels and Millstones: A History of Ohio Gristmills and Milling* and gave numerous presentations on mills in Ohio. He also authored *Jedediah Strong Smith, Fur Trader From Ohio, The Holmes County Rebellion, Tales of the Mohican* and others.

Over the next seventy years, Wesley collected all sorts of material on Naylor, corresponded at length with Naylor's daughter, Lucile, in Malta, Ohio, and made numerous visits there to interview her. During one of these visits Wesley commissioned her to copy for him, in her beautiful handwriting, over one hundred of her father's poems, poems that had not appeared in any of his published books of verse. She also prepared a title page, preface, and an index of the poems, intended for later publication, but the document remains the only copy at this time.

In 1970 I became Wesley's "amanuensis"—his favorite word for secretary and a term that long ago fell into disuse. We discovered a common bond immediately. Wesley was a retired Warrant Officer with thirty years service in the U.S. Navy. He retired the year that I was born. At the time my husband was a young Navy Chief serving on board an aircraft carrier off Vietnam. Despite the fifty-year difference between Wesley and me, we never lacked for topics to discuss, and the Navy was a favorite. Wesley and his lovely wife, Vera, were wonderful with my two young children as well.

He worried about my future should something happen to my husband, and he encouraged me to pursue some sort of career. Because I had expressed an interest in writing and loved doing research, he enlisted my assistance on his Naylor project. We went to Ohio, where we visited the Ohio Historical Society in Columbus and the Kate Love Simpson Library in McConnelsville. We interviewed Naylor's daughter Lucile, his son Robert's widow Edith Naylor, and Robert Wetherell, an elderly cousin. In Zanesville, we met Norris Schneider, a newspaperman who interviewed Naylor and wrote a number of lengthy articles about him. In the San Francisco Bay area, we met and interviewed Naylor's youngest daughter, Jean Finley, on several occasions. She allowed us complete access to all the material about her father in her possession; several large scrapbooks of newspaper articles, short stories, reviews, poems, photographs, and unpublished items. Included in this material were Naylor's handwritten diaries for 1907, and 1916 through 1931 that I later transcribed.

Wesley's unique talent for conducting interviews and gleaning the essence from volumes of research material served as a priceless example for me. His uncanny ability to ask just the right questions encouraged people to open up, and he listened carefully. Over the next year, as I reviewed and cataloged the material, I was inspired by what I was learning about Naylor. I recognized the beginning of one small parallel in Naylor's life and my own in the mentoring that Wesley was giving to me, just as a teacher had done for Naylor. My personal interest in the project was obvious to Wesley, and he suggested that I write the biography of this Ohio legend. Aware of his fondness for the Naylor project and of his failing health, I knew how difficult it was for him to turn his treasure over to me. I felt immensely honored as well as humbled, inadequate, and downright scared that I might not do it justice.

With Wesley's personal mentoring and my own fascination with Naylor to guide me, I spent the next several years preparing what I hoped would be a creditable biography. There was so much material to sift through, and I had an active family, with so many distractions, including more than one move halfway across the country. It was almost like starting over when I found time to return to the project.

The first move put a damper on Wesley's involvement, as did his failing health. Many times the project threatened to overwhelm me, but I learned to narrow my focus and continue on until I had a completed manuscript ready for submission to a publisher. Although deeply disappointed when it was rejected, I was far more distressed at letting Wesley down. With his typical wry sense of humor, he let me know that it was my choice whether this would be a minor distraction or an overwhelming obstacle.

I chose to treat it as a distraction, but before long life threw in more than one overwhelming obstacle in its place. Caring for my mother during a lengthy terminal illness, followed by Wesley's death not long after, was devastating. I put the project on the back burner where it simmered over the next twenty years. During those years, I cared for my family, joined the workforce, earned a college degree, and started my own business.

For too long, the book remained unfinished business that clamored for my time and attention. In 2007, with the help and unwavering support of my husband, Gerry, I returned to the project and started again by cataloging, organizing, and digitizing much of the material. We traveled to Ohio, adding even more material to what was already a comprehensive collection of books, articles, and other data relating to Naylor's life.

As I delved further into the material, I was compelled to find the answer to why Naylor had risen to such dazzling heights of popularity, only to fade into obscurity. In the process, I discovered the "story" of

Naylor's life in his commitment to his family, the importance to him of his role as a country doctor, and in his passion for poetry, writing, and life in general.

Once more engrossed in the material, I began to see so clearly that Naylor's life was not just a collection of facts to be pieced together. The essence of who he was emerged for me. I discovered in Naylor an exceptionally confident man who approached life head on. He lived life on his own terms, making choices for himself and his family that ultimately denied him the long lasting fame and fortune that other writers of that period enjoyed.

Along the way, I learned more than just a bit about myself. I now truly understand that the journey is as important as the destination. How fulfilling it is, after all these years, to have found my "voice," one that Wesley knew was there all along. In doing so, I hope that a new generation of readers will be drawn to the works of this fascinating man and be inspired by his story.

1
The Delectable Days of Childhood

How many of us can look back and clearly see those moments that changed our lives forever or recall even one individual who transformed it by their presence. James Ball Naylor remembered clearly the moment when someone changed his life forever. To him that significant moment when he was sixteen was crystal clear. And it would not be the only defining moment of his life. During his most formative years, two influential men would have a deep and lasting effect on his character, each in their own forceful way. Another powerful man, Warren G. Harding, would severely affect his life in later years. Until that first encounter at the age of sixteen, Naylor enjoyed every moment as a healthy, robust child, unaware of all the promises life held for him.

James Ball Naylor, known from his birth as Jim, was born October 4, 1860, less than a year before the Civil War erupted. He grew up in the center of Morgan County in southeastern Ohio. The village of Malta, nestled along the west side of the Muskingum River across from McConnelsville, the county seat, is still a sleepy village. The river continues to thread its course from Zanesville in the north past Malta and McConnelsville, then southeast to Stockport and on to Marietta where it joins the Ohio River. The hills bordering the river valley are high and precipitous, crowned with trees and fertile land. In the 1860s, steamboats navigating the river were slowed at intervals by a series of dams and locks. The river connected the communities of southeastern Ohio to each other and to the rest of the country.

Theresa Marie Flaherty

High on Newton Ridge, halfway between Malta and Stockport[1] and less than a half mile west of the river, stood the farm of his hardworking parents Robert W. and Nancy (Wells) Naylor. Robert Naylor and his family were Quakers who opposed slavery. His parents, Samuel and Abigail (Ball) Naylor, migrated from Pennsylvania and were among the early Quaker settlers of Penn township. Robert's willingness to fight for the Union cause brought him into conflict with the church. When he enlisted in September, 1861, in Company H, 17th Regiment, Ohio Volunteer Infantry, he was promptly removed from the Quaker church rolls. On November 25, 1863, he was wounded in the battle of Mission Ridge, and died eleven days later at Chattanooga, Tennessee. He was only 27.[2]

Jim's father left before his first birthday and died shortly after his third birthday. Jim was too young to remember him, but his mother and grandmothers did their best to keep his father's memory alive. As a boy, he was deeply affected by the circumstances of his father's death. His mother frequently recounted the story of a treasured family memory. She had given her husband a handmade, heart-shaped valentine addressed "This is my answer, to Bob—from Nan." For two years he carried it in his uniform pocket where it was found, stained with blood, when he

Figure 1.1 - Robert W. Naylor.
Courtesy of Robert Wetherell.

Figure 1.2- Jim Naylor as a child.
Courtesy of Robert Wetherell.

died. When it was returned to her with his other belongings, she discovered that he had added "This is my farewell From Bob to Nan."[3]

Figure 1.3 - Naylor's Birthplace. Courtesy of Jean Naylor Finley.

Figure 1.4 - Farm Buildings. Courtesy of Jean Naylor Finley.

Theresa Marie Flaherty

Their home was a cabin of hewn logs with a roof of rough shingles and a chimney of stones covering one end. Nearby, weathered log farm buildings stood facing the hard-packed dusty road leading up from Bald Eagle creek. Although in Penn township, the farm was within fifty feet of its junction with Windsor and Malta townships. Jim lived out his entire life within these three townships.

Jim's early years were marked by the misery that resulted from the war, but his was only one of countless families to endure the shock and anguish of losing a father, brother, or son. The Newton Ridge neighborhood alone was "completely stripped of its young manhood." Thirty-nine men from sixteen families left to go to war. Six did not return.[4] His mother, struggling to make a scant living for herself and her young son, worked for neighbors as a domestic, as well as doing a man's work on their farm.[5] She put on overalls, rolled up her sleeves and plowed fields, sowed and reaped, and did what needed to be done.[6] Her mother, Nancy (Fouts) Wells, and Ruth Henery,[7] an aunt, took care of Jim. Only the barest necessities were within their means. Coffee, tea, and sugar, though common staples, were far too expensive for them. Jim was fond of bread and milk, but milk was a luxury they seldom enjoyed. More often than not, it was water sweetened with sorghum molasses that quenched his thirst and took the edge off his hunger.

His Grandmother Wells was extremely superstitious. In the evenings as they sat before the fire, she told marvelous witch tales and ghost stories. He teased her by violating her pet taboos, such as whistling on Sunday—a rash act that she considered wicked; but she loved her grandson dearly, and to Jim she was goodness personified. Although reading and writing were profound mysteries to his illiterate grandmother, she was deeply religious and "believed the Book from kiver to kiver."[8]

After the Civil War, when Jim was six, his mother married John B. Henery, a local farmer who was also a Civil War veteran. Jim admired his stepfather, but he revealed very little in his writings of the effect the marriage had on him as a child. The couple was blessed with seven children, six boys and one girl.[9] Jim loved each new addition to the family, but preferred to spend his free time alone or with boys his own age in the outdoors.

His stepfather seemed to have an irresistible urge for moving. As a youngster Jim lived in five different log houses in the circumscribed neighborhood on Newton Ridge. Some of the houses were comfortable, others were not. One was so poorly protected against the elements that almost every winter morning he awoke with snow piled upon the covers of his bed in the loft, snow that had sifted through the warped clapboards.

The changing seasons transformed the valley and altered the pattern of life. At threshing time Jim often watched in fascination as Henry Outcalt and George Bole, neighbors who hired out at threshing time, moved into the countryside with a threshing machine that had five revolving "sweeps" and ten horses. He bribed them with apples or other fruit to let him ride on the platform of the dusty, vibrating thresher or to ride a horse to the watering trough at the noon hour.

Bald Eagle Creek was a small stream, yet large enough for Jim, even as a young boy, to build dams and spend hours swimming and exploring its length. As late as 1867 or 1868, three sawmills were located on the creek within a short distance from his home. One of the mills was owned and operated by "Mur" Scott, his uncle. His cousins, "Err" and Oscar Scott, were playmates, aiding and abetting in all kinds of boyish mischief. When his uncle was not looking, the boys daringly rode the logs as they moved toward the steel teeth of the saw, jumping to safety at the last moment.

On Wolf Creek, west of Stockport, stood the Sauter gristmill, the inspiration for one of Naylor's favorite poems, "The Gray Old Sauter Mill." It stood just below the dam, half of it overhanging the water below and separated by an archway through which the public highway ran. Jim was intrigued by the flour-dusted nooks and crannies and the pleasant sounds of old mills. Each visit whet his appetite for more, and at every opportunity he explored what was to him "the wonder-house of the universe."[10]

There were numerous other gristmills along the streams throughout the area. His stepfather frequented one at Stockport and Jim often accompanied him. Lanky Old Nell was saddled, a bag of grain tossed across the pummel, and Jim was boosted up behind it for the trip. The town boys were always there to greet them, for Nell made "more noise than a caterpillar tractor racing over cobblestones," and never failed to give away their approach long before they reached the village. It was an experience never forgotten.[11]

Theresa Marie Flaherty

Figure 1.5 - Stockport Mill.

Naylor recalls being out in the field with his stepfather, a Civil war veteran and staunch Republican, when a neighbor, Thomas D. Clancy, approached, excited over a big Republican rally scheduled at McConnelsville. The presidential campaign was in full swing, and excitement was at fever pitch. Each township was expected to send a delegation, and Henery's help was needed in getting a wagonload of people from their neighborhood into town.

"We've got to vote and work as we shot, John!" Clancy said.

Henery, a man of few words, assured him, "Tom, we'll be on hand." [12]

Early the next morning the rumbling wagons with their load of potential voters gathered at Stockport. Heavy fog still hung over the river; there was no bridge, and it took more than two hours to ferry all the vehicles across. When they rolled into McConnelsville, flags were waving and the drum corps was creating great excitement. Men whooped, woman waved, and children added to the furor.

For the country lad, it was a momentous occasion. "I shall never forget that political gathering," Naylor wrote:

> For one reason—because I was but eight years old; and had never dreamed of such a gorgeous panorama—had never thought that there could be so many people, flags and banners, horses and vehicles, in the whole wide world. For another reason—because I took ague a few days afterward; and every time the chill deserted me, I saw the entire thing over and over again; and babbled of it, incoherently.[13]

Sickness and death were common occurrences when Jim was a boy. Women died in childbirth, and childhood diseases claimed many lives. During the summer mosquitoes multiplied in swamps and marshes in great numbers, and malaria was rife. Jim suffered bouts of chills and fever and, when he was ten years old, he came down with both measles and malaria and nearly died.

His mother and grandmother, like most farm wives, relied on home remedies and provided nursing care for all but the most serious problems. A doctor, called only as a last resort, often traveled many miles to reach a patient. His visit was a big event in the eyes of a child, particularly to young Jim.

Dr. James W. White, of Stockport, was the first doctor Jim remembered who had come to their home to care for him. Feverish, restless and peevish, Jim tossed and turned, half asleep when he heard the doctor's voice.

"I was so well peppered that my face resembled that of a Chinese god," he recalled. "Half asleep, I heard a voice say 'Why he's got the measles.'"

Jim sensed immediately that the doctor was a kindly man. He liked the man's luxuriant whiskers, but thought that he wore the oddest trousers he had ever seen. He saw at once that they were very muddy. What Jim mistook for trousers were actually thigh-length leggings, buttoned down the sides. While the doctor was preparing some medicine for him to take, Jim piped up inquisitively, "Doctor, why don't you take off your pants and clean 'em?"[14]

Jim recalled, "Peals of laughter followed, of course. Dr. White sat and chuckled, and wheezed—and shook like the proverbial bowl of jelly; and I, confused and offended, turned my face to the wall."[15]

Jim was a country boy through and through, and the boys in Stockport did not let him forget it. On his infrequent trips to the market for his mother, the boys teased and pestered him; and more than once ran him out of town. When his family eventually moved into a ramshackle house at the upper end of Stockport for a while, there was an inevitable confrontation. The village boys taunted him, calling repeatedly, "Jim Naylor's a country jake."[16] In the tussle that followed he emerged with a black eye, "a badge of courage, to be valued above rubies" from the battle that followed.[17]

His mother took one look at him and demanded an explanation. When he gave it, she laughed, "Well, I don't get moved into town—till you've got moved in and had a fight!" Then, her tone turning somber, she said, "Jim, I know what it means for you. You've got no bigger brothers to help you; you'll have to fight your own battles—take your own part."[18]

And fight he did, as boys and men then were likely to do; but he was a gregarious ten-year old, and soon he was accepted by the barefoot boys. Together they hunted, in summer they swam, in winter they skated on the frozen river, and few orchards escaped their visitations.

Most of the village boys had bats and balls, but not Jim, so he traded a peck of walnuts for a bat and appealed to his mother for a ball. She unraveled some cast-off woolen socks for the yarn and tore up an old rubber shoe for the elastic material and fashioned the ball. It was a good piece of handiwork, but it lacked a leather cover. "You find me some leather; and I'll try the thing," she said. "I can't do worse than fail."

Jim remembered seeing a pile of leather cuttings inside the door of the village saddler's shop, so he hurried over, went inside, and began to search through them. When the saddler, with iron gray hair and whiskers and a kindly expression, asked what he was doing, Jim replied, "I'm trying to find a piece of leather big enough to cover a ball."

The saddler said, "Let me have the ball." Taking it, he began to make a cover himself.

Thinking the saddler would ask to be paid, Jim suddenly felt sick. He had no money. He said, "I'm aw-awful glad to have the ball covered; but I haven't got—got any money to pay you."

The saddler laughed at Jim's response, "Well, who in the world asked you for money—or expected money, hey?" said the saddler, adding, "Run along and play now," as he tossed Jim the finished ball.

The saddler's kindness was never forgotten, and years later Naylor traveled to a country fair a dozen miles away because he heard that his old friend would be there. He searched the grounds until he found his benefactor and, with tears in his eyes, he shook the hand of the tottering old man.[19]

Occasionally, he went to Malta to visit the families of his Aunt Lydia Manly and Aunt Ruth Hughes. On one trip when he was ten or twelve years old, he went up to the plow factory with a half dozen of his friends. Each found a long, thin, pliable strip of wood that had been ripped from heavy wood. The boys jumped astride their makeshift stick-horses and took off, whooping and yelling down the street. They encountered Dr. Wood, a dignified gentleman wearing a long coat and a tall silk hat. The other boys, in passing the doctor, brushed his legs with their stick-horses. Jim resolved to do one better. He jumped off his nimble nag and was going to sweep it high over the doctor's head, but he miscalculated. The stick struck the silk hat, sending it rolling into the muddy street.

"Hey there, boy!" Dr. Wood shouted angrily. "If I catch you, I'll skite you!"[20]

Jim had no idea what "skite" meant, but thought murder might be appropriate. The boys all dashed away. After that, when the boys went into the doctor's drug store to sell the bottles they had gathered from the old wooden bridge, Jim stayed safely outside, letting his friends handle the transaction.

Years later, when his first book of verse was published, he sent an autographed copy to Dr. Wood and included a letter "informing him that the author of the verses was the grown up pest that had sent his hat bowling in the muddy street."[21] Dr. Wood wrote back saying that he recalled the incident and that his anger had quickly dissipated, and he had laughed about it.

Despite the austerity that marked his early years, Jim fully enjoyed life. In reminiscing, he called those days "the dear, delectable days of childhood, of boyhood—of sunshiny and soul-satisfying youth!"[22] He was, in his own words, "a young savage—frank and admirable, impish and impossible."[23]

Among his warmest childhood memories were the days spent outdoors running wild and free. With a thumb hooked through his only suspender and a battered hat perched jauntily on his head, he wandered barefoot through the woods bent upon discovery. Newton Ridge, with its many forested areas along the river, was a constant attraction, because it was here that Jim hunted squirrels and rabbits, fished, and enjoyed listening to the sounds of nature. He learned the names and habits of the animals and could identify the trees and plants of the Muskingum Valley, his great love. His knowledge of its natural wonders and appreciation for its beauties deepened as he grew older, providing inspiration that found expression in poetry and prose.

The Bailey Church was Methodist and Jim remembered vividly the "Big Meetings" that were held there in the winter. Sleds and sleighs and saddle horses lined both sides of the little highway and their owners crowded into the old building, filling all the pews and standing in the aisles and even around the pulpit.

"Reverend Hathaway was a big man, physically, and a revivalist hard to excel. He arose in the pulpit. His bald head, sunk between massive shoulders, almost touched the ceiling; his luxuriant beard swept his waist."[24] A typical died-in-the-wool fundamentalist, he thumped the Bible and stamped the pulpit as he preached his sermon of death and darkness and the devil. Naylor recalled many times wending his way home from those emotional meetings with "chills playing tag up and down my spine, for I was an unregenerate young sinner."[25]

Apparently unsuccessful at his occupation in Stockport, Jim's stepfather once again returned to a farm on Newton Ridge. The farm overlooked the Muskingum River, where Jim spent many happy hours watching the steamboats travel up and down the river. On many summer nights the musical whistle of a steamboat, resonant and far reaching,

Figure 1.6 - Packet Boat at the dock in Malta. Courtesy of the Morgan County Historical Society.

sounded across the hills from Stockport as the boat blew for the village locks, stirring Jim's vivid imagination and arousing hopes that one day he might become a steamboatsman. His uncle Taylor Wells was a pilot on the Ohio and Mississippi Rivers for many years. Although Jim never met him, the family talked so much about his life as a steamboatsman that Uncle Taylor became his idol.

At the age of twelve, Jim went to Stockport and tried to coax Tom Clancy, a steward on one of the packets, to employ him as a cabin boy. Tom said kindly, "I've promised a place to Kinney Abbott; but you be here when we come back down the river. If Kinney doesn't take the place, you can have it."[26] Jim was waiting on the wharf with his bundle when the packet returned from Zanesville. The other boy was nowhere in sight. Jim was ecstatic. But just at the last possible moment, as the boat was ready to pull out, Kinney strutted aboard, dashing Jim's dream. A career as a steamboatsman ended before it ever had a chance to begin.

Much of the attraction was the opportunity to get away from the work that was part of his life in the valley. The following winter he stayed with his Uncle Alvanus and Aunt Ruth Henery at their home a mile above Hooksburg on the river. When one of their children became ill, his Uncle Van skated on the river for more than six miles to McConnelsville, bringing back a doctor, also on skates.[27] Jim was quite impressed.

He attended school six months each year, and during vacation he worked from four in the morning till eight at night on the farm that his stepfather rented, carrying water, chopping and toting wood, driving and milking the cows, feeding the pigs, hunting eggs, watering the horses, hoeing in the garden, and running errands. He worked, although grudgingly. "I toiled simply to obtain immunity from sharp rebukes and was looked upon as a lazy incorrigible."[28]

The first money he earned was working for a neighboring farmer at twenty-five cents a day. Tobacco was raised in the area and for three seasons, from the age of thirteen until sixteen, he "helped in the production of this 'filthy weed.'"[29] He picked blackberries and hauled eggs and other products to market. He also remembered "loitering all day long in a cornfield—the blue and cloudless sky above me, the bright sunlight flecking my torn hat's jaunty brim—doing nothing, nothing in the world but wielding a hoe and smiting the foxtail grass from the path of the growing corn."[30]

Jim attended the one-room Newton Ridge school in Windsor township from the time he was five until he was seventeen, with the exception of one winter term in Stockport. During the winter months he attended school regularly, but in the summer work at home prevented him from attending more than just occasionally. Confined to a classroom with summer in the air was more than he could have endured. "I was an idle dreamer, without aid or ambition, caring more for the fields and woods than for the lessons between a textbook," he said.[31]

The school was ungraded. Each pupil made his own decision as to what he wished to study. Reading, writing, spelling, and arithmetic were the choices of most pupils and their parents. Jim disliked school intensely, but even then his way with words was remarkable, and he recalled getting into trouble almost daily because of comic poems he penned and passed about the room. Clearly, he enjoyed being the center of attention. Disrupting the one-room schoolhouse class with his poetic efforts often resulted in dire consequences for him. He never forgot the many "scutchings" he received and recalled them without feelings of animosity. It was a small price to pay for the growing warmth and recognition that he received from his peers.

"I wrote comic verses, passed them around and got pupils to laughing. Then came the licking. Next day I'd write another."[32] He later wrote a short story, "The Diversions of Dicky Dare," about just such a boy. Dicky wrote an uncomplimentary poem about the teacher, causing much amusement to the rest of the boys. The teacher, demanding to know the cause of the commotion, ordered Dicky to recite it for him. Dicky quickly changed the words so that it came out complimentary, so complimentary in fact, that he was asked to recite it for a gathering of parents at school. To do so would have endangered his standing with his friends, so he again changed the words, much to the embarrassment of the teacher and his lady love, but not enough to incur the teacher's wrath. No one knows whether Jim actually accomplished a similar feat, but considering his quick wit and ease with a rhyme, it is certainly possible.

During those early, carefree years he absorbed the marvelous sights and melodic rhythms of the countryside, filing them away and later recalling them with a sweetness and intensity that touched those who read his poems and stories.

2
What are you going to be?

 Who knows what might have become of the aimless, drifting young man without the intervention of James M. Rusk, whom Naylor credits with changing his outlook on life. Rusk was a new teacher who arrived in the fall of 1876 when Naylor was sixteen and most in need of a guiding hand. He continued to serve as the young man's mentor through the most formative years of his life. Blessed with a keen insight into boyish nature, Rusk sparked Naylor's interest in learning. Attracted by the teacher's warmth and attention, Naylor quickly realized that Rusk was different from any teacher he had ever known. Although a strict disciplinarian, Rusk was also a kind and gentle man who understood his pupils.

 Quick to recognize Naylor's latent talent, Rusk took an interest in the awkward teenager, rousing him out of his daydreaming. Rusk later wrote about his perceptions of the young man he had discovered and encouraged:

> Seventy pupils presented themselves on commencement morning, ranging in age from little six year old tots to full grown men and women. Among that number was a lad of marked individuality, bilious, nervous temperament, keen-eyed, and as I afterwards discovered, possessed of the keenest intellect of the entire group. From the first this pupil was a favorite. Eager to learn, studious, methodical and docile, he won the teacher's heart, and the ties of friendship were formed which have run

down through the years to the present. I soon discovered that the boy was not without ambition; but up to that time in his life whatever ambition he had, remained potential, had not taken on current force, had not found an outlet or channel.[33]

Until that time Naylor had thought little about his future, assuming he would become a farmer like his stepfather. Rusk made him aware of his own potential for the first time in his life. "I was one of his pupils, a 16-year-old backwoods youth, without aim or ambition—my one redeeming virtue being my love for books, good, bad, and indifferent."[34]

One noon hour after only a week of teaching, Rusk called him aside and posed a disconcerting question, "What are you going to be when you get to be a man?"[35] That fateful moment was the spark that changed his life.

To this abrupt question the young boy answered, "A farmer, I suppose."[36]

Rusk pointed out that he was physically unsuited to being a farmer. He told the boy to get himself a *Greene's Grammar*, and if he would apply himself diligently and attend the upper school in Stockport the next year, he would see that he obtained a teaching position.

Before that time, Naylor was too busy thinking about a good time. Whatever else Rusk said during that crucial talk inspired the youth.

> He took an interest in me and even roused me, to some extent, out of my dreaminess. He showed me the usefulness of exact knowledge; he taught me the beauties of literature, he fired me with ambition; he brought me books to read—Ivanhoe, Robinson Crusoe, Dickens novels, and I eagerly devoured them. My taste aroused, became an unquenchable thirst. Our library at home consisted of a Bible, a Methodist hymnal, and an Ayer's Almanac. I set out on a quest for books to read, I scoured the countryside, all was fish that came to my net.[37]

Rusk eventually closed the school and went away, but he left an indelible mark on the impressionable young man, by creating within him a desire for knowledge and a need for self-expression. Resolved to have an education, Naylor promised Rusk that he would put it to good use. In his own words, he said, "I have kept the faith—the promise I made him."[38]

As a student at Stockport's ungraded high school for seven months, he learned the fundamentals and explored the wonders of literature in the books he borrowed. Hoping to acquire a classic education, he attended Marietta Academy for five months in 1879. He borrowed money for tuition from John McDermott, a Stockport merchant, and to earn extra money for expenses, he tutored other students, among them Rufus R. Dawes, who became a national banker and industrialist and president of the Century of Progress Exposition in Chicago for the 1933 World's Fair, and his brother Charles, who served as vice president under Calvin Coolidge. Naylor and the brothers would remain life-long friends.[39]

When financial circumstances prevented Naylor from returning to Marietta, Rusk helped him secure a teaching position in a country school near Malta starting at a dollar and a quarter for a day's work. A good teacher, Naylor was known for his ability to tame the older boys in the same way Rusk had taught him, through kindness and humor. He taught three successive winter terms at the Wetherell school, Malta township—on top of Doudna Hill.[40] He taught in the district schools in Morgan County for a total of five years during the winters and worked on farms during the summer months. Although he loved teaching, the daily upkeep of the school was physically demanding, as was the added pressure he put upon himself because he wanted to return to Marietta Academy. From the strain, he developed nervous indigestion that plagued him for the rest of his life.

Little is known about the years he taught. Although his desire to accomplish something worthwhile was earnest, he had no fixed goals and he lacked maturity. Outgoing and with many friends, he had few responsibilities beyond the classroom. Quick-tempered and prone to reacting physically, just as he did as a boy, he often fought over insignificant matters, once pitching a man who insulted him through a window. No doubt he inherited his temperament from his mother, who belonged to the Wells family. "They had plenty of horse sense and keen intellects, but were not in the least bookish," he said. "You could not tread on the tails of their coats or the toes of their shoes without having a fight. Man or woman, they'd fight."[41]

With the same zest for life and penchant for discovery displayed as a boy, Naylor, as a young man, flexed his attitudes as well as his muscles. Determined to discover the honors and pleasures of reaching manhood, he discovered its follies as well. However, he did emerge from those awkward years as a stable individual.

Besides being physically challenging, teaching stifled his own desire to learn. Naylor turned to medicine where pharmacy aroused his curiosity and interest. Friends scoffed at his lofty aspirations, saying that he was better suited to farming. His stepfather suggested that he invest his money in land. Nevertheless, Naylor persisted.

When Dr. Wesley Emmet Gatewood, fifteen years his senior, hired him as a clerk in his drug store in Stockport, the course of Naylor's life was once again altered. Gatewood began his medical practice in Stockport in June, 1876, when he graduated from Dartmouth Medical College in New Hampshire. Because he was tireless in his efforts and energy, his practice expanded quickly. He considered himself "self-reliant, imperious and persistent, with an aggressive nature and a hereditary fixity of purpose that tolerates no intervention."[42] Yet he felt that "the austerity of his nature" was softened by warm and generous impulses. He must have been a hard man for he asked and made no concessions, and "when compelled to break off friendships tears up the bridge to prevent its return."[43] That Naylor thrived under this man is a testament to his own character.

Gatewood provided more than the foundation for Naylor's professional

Figure 2.1 - Wesley Emmet Gatewood

life as a country doctor. He also provided the cornerstone for his steadfast beliefs and moral code as well. Realizing Naylor's potential, he began to teach him the fundamentals of his profession. A fiery and independent thinker, Gatewood was not an easy taskmaster, but Naylor respected him and soon earned his respect. Among other things, Gatewood was well known as a "cheerful conversationalist of fertile fancy, vigorous imagination and fair memory: a severe, unsparing satirist, indulging in an unfortunate fondness for scathing sarcasm or keenest irony."[44] An apt student of more than just medicine, Naylor impressed the doctor with his determination and ability. His curiosity extended to all phases of the physician's work, and Gatewood quickly recognized his intelligence and decided that Naylor would make a fine doctor.

For assisting in the drug store for two summers, Gatewood paid Naylor's expenses at Starling Medical College in Columbus for two terms. The requirements for admission at that time were that a candidate be of good moral character and have a high school diploma or teaching certificate. In addition, medical students secured part of their training as

Figure 2.2 - Gatewood's Drug Store in Stockport.

an apprentice to a practicing physician. Naylor, one of at least six young men who studied medicine under Gatewood, was fortunate to work for a man who was both a physician with a large practice, and a pharmacist. After two six-month terms of lectures, dissections, laboratory work and hospital experience, he was ready for his final examination.[45] Naylor received his degree on March 4, 1886, graduating second in a class of eighty-one.[46]

The influence of both Rusk and Gatewood left an enduring mark on Naylor, but his own strength of character, his determination, and the force of his own emerging personality allowed him to determine what traits, qualities, and beliefs he would cultivate to guide his own destiny.

On March 28, 1886, two weeks after graduating from Starling Medical College, Naylor returned to Stockport and married Myrta Gibson, the daughter of Captain C. J. Gibson, a prominent Stockport merchant. Six weeks later he opened his practice there.[47]

"After graduation" he said, "I hung out my shingle in Babylon [Stockport], and practiced there one fleeting year—spending most of my working hours in a wet saddle. The good people of the community bore with me—and charitably excused my woeful inexperience."[48]

One of the most traumatic and heartbreaking episodes in his life occurred in little more than a year when his young bride contracted tuberculosis. Despite all his training as a physician, he was unable to do much more than to make her comfortable. She clung to life for several months with little hope of recovery. She died on June 18, 1887[49]. A report in a local newspaper reported, "Though so young and hopeful, she bore her sufferings with entire resignation, fully

Figure 2.3 - Naylor with a Beard.
Courtesy of D. W. Garber.

trusting in the savior, who has taken her to the many mansioned house on high."[50] Naylor quickly abandoned his efforts to establish a practice in Stockport and became a traveling salesman for Park Davis, a Detroit drug firm, "toting grip" for several months until he regained his perspective.[51]

He returned to Pennsville, and on August 6, 1888, he married Lena Ervilla Naylor, a distant cousin. After this marriage at the age of twenty-eight, Naylor was ready to settle down and establish himself as a country doctor among the people he knew growing up. He and Villa moved into a small, one-room house in Pennsville, a country village not far from Newton Ridge. Their little home was so small that Villa kept the dishes under the bed, and she sat on the edge of it to cook. Between them they had only ten dollars. Still, "they laughed and sang their way through poverty and pinch until he could get his medical practice established...."[52]

Figure 2.4 - Lena Ervilla Naylor in 1886.
Courtesy of Lucile Naylor.

Villa waited patiently for his arrival each evening, looking forward to their time together to enjoy the evening meal and discuss the day's events.

Villa was his helpmate right from the beginning, even learning how to "roll pills" for him.[53] The youngest in a large family of twelve children, five of them step-brothers and step-sisters, she grew up working hard and loving it. Keeping up a small house and caring just for herself and her husband was an easy task for someone so used to hard work. John Thompson Leslie Naylor, her father, was a carpenter and cabinet maker and Olivia Ellen (Coulson) Naylor, her mother, was a seamstress and milliner.[54] While her older siblings helped to make a living for the family, she stayed home and did the housework. Included among those chores was washing clothes in a large tub, scrubbing them on a washboard with homemade soap.

One wash-day, her next older sister came by to help, wearing a neatly starched dress. Villa, strong and high-spirited with a wonderful sense of humor, picked her up and dumped her into a tub of water, as both screeched and hollered. The sisters loved to tell the story, laughing together as they recounted it.[55]

For Naylor, establishing a medical practice in Pennsville was not an easy undertaking, and collecting fees was even more difficult. In an era when the purchasing power of a dollar went a very long way, a house call was only twenty-five cents. If the patient required treatment or medicine, another fifty cents was added. For an examination, the charge was two dollars and fifty cents. For obstetrical cases that later comprised a large portion of his practice, Naylor usually charged from two dollars and fifty cents to eight dollars; although in one instance, he charged seven dollars and fifty cents for delivering twins.[56] Consultations were usually fifty cents, but for a night visit that got him up and out of bed, it was three dollars.

Although it was not his specialty, occasionally he was called upon to perform surgery in emergency situations. His fee ranged from twenty-five cents to fifteen dollars, depending on its nature. The operation usually was done on the kitchen table with a member of the household giving the anesthetic. For less urgent surgeries, Naylor referred his patients

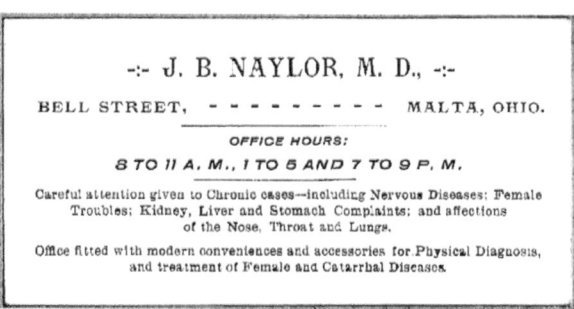

Figure 2.5 - Naylor's Business Card. Courtesy of Greg and Ellen Hill.

to a surgeon in Zanesville or Columbus, often accompanying them and giving the anesthesia. As was true of most physicians of that era, he also pulled teeth; however, this was not a favorite part of his practice. He referred patients to a dentist when one was available.

Because money was scarce, bartering was common. His patients, often unable to pay in cash, exchanged labor, produce, feed for his horse, or other commodity in payment. A. H. Matson, the blacksmith, paid most of his account by shoeing Naylor's horse. Mr. Dickerson, who ran the livery stable, paid his bill by keeping the doctor's horse at six dollars a month, while another patient, George Naylor, exchanged books on geometry and physics for his one dollar and fifty cent bill. "The only case on record, doubtless, of physics being dispensed from patient to doctor."[57] In one instance he even accepted ten cents on account for "tinkering with pipe."[58]

A. W. Walker paid his bill in tailor-made clothes, "By overcoat—$27.00, by suit—$29.00, By hat—$2.50."[59] Naylor, a tall, slender man, took care with his appearance and Villa always kept his clothes neatly pressed. By bartering, he was able to dress well, but sustaining his family on his early meager income was challenging. Fortunately, many patients bartered with meat and other staples, and Naylor supplemented his earnings by picking chickens and shooting and cleaning rabbits to sell.[60]

No matter how small the bill, there were patients who objected. One man's wife, who was in poor health already, contracted typhoid fever and became desperately ill. Naylor made numerous trips out to the farm to treat her, and she eventually recovered. When a neighbor commented on their good fortune, the husband replied testily, "Yes, but it cost the price of one good cow!"[61]

The Naylor's cramped quarters in the little house in Pennsville seemed smaller still after the birth of their first child, Olive Nance, on May 12, 1889. Two years later, in 1891 when a second baby was imminent, they moved eight miles north to Malta to an apartment in the Beckworth Building over the general store owned by A. A. Coulson, Villa's second cousin.

While preparing to move, the family stayed in the Methodist parsonage. There, on November 4, 1891, an election day, their second

Figure 2.6 - The Naylors' Apartment over the Coulson Store. Courtesy of Norris F. Schneider.

daughter, Nettie Lucile, was born. Her birth kept her father, who was keenly interested in politics, from watching the returns being posted at the telegraph office at the Baltimore and Ohio railroad station. In later years it became a standing joke in the family. He often teased Lucile, saying he "never liked her" because of it, when, in fact, he was devoted to her.

Naylor moved his practice to Malta where he prospered. He continued to make house calls to his scattered clientele in the hill country of Morgan County as his practice in town grew. One of his patients was a farmer whose jaw was easily dislocated. When this happened, the farmer quickly mounted his horse and rode to Malta. Even before jumping from his horse, he cried out in a rasping voice, loud enough for Naylor to hear. Knowing at once what was wrong, Naylor grabbed a clean towel to wrap around the man's face. With his fingers, he quickly snapped the jaw back into place and the farmer gratefully headed back home.[62]

One room in the apartment above the Coulson store served as Naylor's office, but he did not see many patients there. Patients who felt well enough to travel into town probably felt they did not need to see a doctor. Consequently, his early practice consisted mostly of house calls. Naylor visited his patients on horseback or in a small one-horse shay, unless they were in town. Then he walked.

The railroad did not come to Morgan County until December, 1886, and the first automobiles did not appear until after the turn of the century. Malta was a river town and the river area, where stores, warehouse, wharf, and depot were located, was a bustling center of activity for the town. Transportation was limited to riverboat or horseback or horse-drawn conveyances of various sorts or to walking. Roads were well worn paths, often bumpy, muddy, and difficult to follow.

On the long rides to visit patients in winter, the unpaved, narrow, snow-covered country roads could be icy and grueling to travel. Trips became a test of endurance as the numbing cold penetrated even heavy woolen clothing. Once at his destination, Naylor tended his horse before hurrying inside to stand before the blazing hearth for a few minutes, restoring warmth to his weary body. After examining the patient and giving careful instructions for further care, he faced the bitter cold again.

In summer, the valley was at its peak of loveliness, but heat and insects often marred his rides. The sweltering sun would take its toll by the time he returned, exhausted, at home in the evening. Daunting as his travels seem today, it was accepted as a way of life. Naylor's ability as a doctor to nurture his patients and bring comfort provided a satisfying sense of accomplishment at the end of the day.

As a physician, Naylor was widely respected. A tribute to him cited his skill as a diagnostician. "As a physician he possessed all the qualifications to have made his name famous in the medical world. He is exceptionally gifted as a diagnostician and his knowledge and wide range of reading have kept him abreast with every advanced step in the profession."[8]

If his goal in life was to be an able physician, respected in the community for his work, then he succeeded admirably. But for Naylor, it was not enough. He began to write "to satisfy an inward longing..." and "not with any hope of wealth or fame."[63] He wrote because he had to write.

3
S. Q. Lapius Emerges

Naylor drew inspiration from everything and everyone with whom he came into contact. On his solitary rides visiting his patients, ideas for poems and stories were born as his horse plodded along. The poet in him delighted in nature's beauty whatever the season, and he cataloged in memory each lovely scene for later recall. The long rides may have been lonely, but his mind was always active.

His first published poem, "The Muskingum Valley," was about the beauty in his own backyard. During an interview in 1935, he appealed to his wife for the date and she said: "Why, it was in 1889, right after we were married, Daddy. I made you enter the contest. I said you would, you said you wouldn't; then I said you would, and you did."[64]

A reward was offered by none other than Dr. Gatewood for the best poem on the Muskingum Valley. Apparently Naylor was not the only other aspiring poet in the area. Gatewood hoped to "arouse this latent force into action" with the contest. Quite a number competed for this prize, and "several contributions possessed special merit."[65]

Naylor won the ten dollar first prize. The poem appeared in the *McConnelsville Herald* and Naylor's literary career began in earnest. This was his first tangible recognition as a poet, although he had contributed a number of poems to *The Democrat*, a newspaper published in McConnelsville.[66] The only other poem known to have been published that early was "The Little Old Druggist," and it is one of the very few to be signed "J. B. Naylor, M.D."

Naylor's poems, published in area newspapers, were received enthusiastically. Before long, a number of periodicals solicited contributions. Within a very few years, over two hundred poems appeared in print under his pseudonym, S. Q. Lapius, a play on the name of the Roman god of healing, Aesculapius.[67]

Poetry was music to Naylor's soul. To him it was the most important part of his literary life. "I wrote for the joy of writing. The most satisfaction and the greatest treat I ever had was the creation of a poem," he said.[68] "I write poetry for the same reason that I read so much of it; because it seems a part of me, and I cannot help doing it."[69]

In 1893, at the urging of his wife, Naylor published his first collection of poetry, *Current Coins Picked up at a Country Railway Station*. Included among the more than thirty poems were several dialect poems that are among his best. A writer in an early biographical sketch said: "Among these may be mentioned 'In That Ol' Tobacker Patch,' 'My Time O' Year,' 'Pop-Paw Time,' 'The Ol' Fence Row,' 'The Buckwheat Bloom,' 'Jest Lazyin' Round,' 'Hide-an-Seek,' 'Like 'Er Ma,' and many others." He continued, "Some of these are perfect jewels of their kind. In one sense local in their setting, they are universal in the higher sense of depicting the aspirations, the longings and regrets of humanity."[70]

"The Muskingum Valley" appeared in this volume also. By selecting Fannie Hawkins, of McConnelsville, to create the artwork, the entire work was a Morgan County product.

Villa's cousin, A. A. Coulson, agreed to furnish all the necessary funds for publication, according to the hand-written contract between the two of them dated September 2, 1893. After legitimate costs were paid, the net proceeds were to be divided equally between Naylor and Coulson. Hann and Adair, a firm in Columbus, printed one thousand volumes issued as the first and only edition. *Current Coins* was a beautiful volume, handsomely printed and attractively bound, but despite the author's hopeful expectations, the sales were disappointing. Initially priced at a dollar and a half, the volume did not sell well. Many books remained stacked in a corner of the general store beneath his office for a long time after and finally

3

S. Q. Lapius Emerges

Naylor drew inspiration from everything and everyone with whom he came into contact. On his solitary rides visiting his patients, ideas for poems and stories were born as his horse plodded along. The poet in him delighted in nature's beauty whatever the season, and he cataloged in memory each lovely scene for later recall. The long rides may have been lonely, but his mind was always active.

His first published poem, "The Muskingum Valley," was about the beauty in his own backyard. During an interview in 1935, he appealed to his wife for the date and she said: "Why, it was in 1889, right after we were married, Daddy. I made you enter the contest. I said you would, you said you wouldn't; then I said you would, and you did."[64]

A reward was offered by none other than Dr. Gatewood for the best poem on the Muskingum Valley. Apparently Naylor was not the only other aspiring poet in the area. Gatewood hoped to "arouse this latent force into action" with the contest. Quite a number competed for this prize, and "several contributions possessed special merit."[65]

Naylor won the ten dollar first prize. The poem appeared in the *McConnelsville Herald* and Naylor's literary career began in earnest. This was his first tangible recognition as a poet, although he had contributed a number of poems to *The Democrat*, a newspaper published in McConnelsville.[66] The only other poem known to have been published that early was "The Little Old Druggist," and it is one of the very few to be signed "J. B. Naylor, M.D."

Naylor's poems, published in area newspapers, were received enthusiastically. Before long, a number of periodicals solicited contributions. Within a very few years, over two hundred poems appeared in print under his pseudonym, S. Q. Lapius, a play on the name of the Roman god of healing, Aesculapius.[67]

Poetry was music to Naylor's soul. To him it was the most important part of his literary life. "I wrote for the joy of writing. The most satisfaction and the greatest treat I ever had was the creation of a poem," he said.[68] "I write poetry for the same reason that I read so much of it; because it seems a part of me, and I cannot help doing it."[69]

In 1893, at the urging of his wife, Naylor published his first collection of poetry, *Current Coins Picked up at a Country Railway Station*. Included among the more than thirty poems were several dialect poems that are among his best. A writer in an early biographical sketch said: "Among these may be mentioned 'In That Ol' Tobacker Patch,' 'My Time O' Year,' 'Pop-Paw Time,' 'The Ol' Fence Row,' 'The Buckwheat Bloom,' 'Jest Lazyin' Round,' 'Hide-an-Seek,' 'Like 'Er Ma,' and many others." He continued, "Some of these are perfect jewels of their kind. In one sense local in their setting, they are universal in the higher sense of depicting the aspirations, the longings and regrets of humanity."[70]

"The Muskingum Valley" appeared in this volume also. By selecting Fannie Hawkins, of McConnelsville, to create the artwork, the entire work was a Morgan County product.

Villa's cousin, A. A. Coulson, agreed to furnish all the necessary funds for publication, according to the hand-written contract between the two of them dated September 2, 1893. After legitimate costs were paid, the net proceeds were to be divided equally between Naylor and Coulson. Hann and Adair, a firm in Columbus, printed one thousand volumes issued as the first and only edition. *Current Coins* was a beautiful volume, handsomely printed and attractively bound, but despite the author's hopeful expectations, the sales were disappointing. Initially priced at a dollar and a half, the volume did not sell well. Many books remained stacked in a corner of the general store beneath his office for a long time after and finally sold for as little as twenty-five cents. Eventually enough money was earned to pay for the printing, but little profit was ever realized. Today the volume is a rare treasure.

The book was planned in the style of Longfellow's *Tales of a Wayside Inn* and consisted of four "collections" representing the seasons of the year. In his introduction to each, the author wove a description of the beautiful scenery along the Muskingum River as it appeared in the appropriate season.

Figure 3.1 - Malta Railway Station. Courtesy of James W. Mason.

The railway station, located in Malta beside the river near the bridge to McConnelsville, was the locale where characters congregated to tell of their lives, their sorrows, and their beliefs.

Reviews of *Current Coins* were some of the best he ever received. One far-sighted editor wrote:

> It argues for still better things from the pen of Dr. Naylor and marks the opening of a career in literature that if pursued and carried out to the logical sequence that 'Current Coin'

promises means that before long S. Q. Lapius will rank among the literati of Ohio."[71]

Several glowing reviews appeared in newspapers. In one, Professor Byron W. King commented:

> I like them; I like them very much. They have the certain stamp of genius, they are not mere rhymes, but poems. The author will certainly become well and favorably known. They have the marks of originality, and as pieces of character painting I think them of very high order indeed. I shall hope to hear much more from him.[72]

None were more complimentary than the review in the *Zanesville Times Recorder*:

> In the discovery of this hidden jewel among the hills of Morgan county the TIMES RECORDER feels that it has played a part, and it is therefore with pleasure and ill-concealed pride that we announce the appearance of the first collection of his poems in book form.... The pictures you have seen—but only in nature. Here you find them in language which has preserved the tints and shades of coloring which even the artist's brush must have blurred had he attempted to catch them."[73]

After medical school Naylor lost touch with his mentor, Rusk, who had moved to Washington, D. C. where he was Chief of the Agricultural Division of the Census Department.[74] Although Rusk had enjoyed the poetry of S.Q. Lapius, it was not until the poem, "The Little White School House," appeared that Rusk discovered that the poet and his former student were one and the same. He wrote:

> I read it. Then I read it over again. Memory got in its work. I was away from Washington, I was again among the boys and girls and the sunlight of Newton ridge. My face took on color, my eyes yielded to a moistening influence. I was living years agone, over again.[75]

JAMES BALL NAYLOR

Rusk called Naylor's poetry "simply pretty, quaint and beautiful" with a graceful form, and he admired the quaint and eccentric characters Naylor depicted in them.

> Notice how perfect the rhythm of his poems is. Rhythm is the manner of poetry. It is to poetry what grace is to ourselves, our movements. Fitting the rhythm to the language and binding these to the sense is harmony. The power which does this is genius. It is born in the artist. It cannot be acquired.[76]

The dialect poems in the volume were among his best, capturing the essence of the rural characters he described. In the cadence and nuances of their speech he revealed their joys, sorrows, hopes and dreams. His use of dialect was "impeccable" and brought many favorable responses.[77] He was especially pleased when compared with other contemporaries, including Edward Guest, Will Carleton, and James Whitcomb Riley, who all became his personal friends.

Naylor was very careful in selecting poems appropriate for each volume of collected verse, and he had a wide range of subjects from which to choose. No subject was immune to his poetry, particularly his own profession. In 1894 he took a facetious look into the next century in "A Peep into the Medical Future," making several amazing predictions. In this poem, one that does

Figure 3.2 - The Country Doctor.

not appear in any of his books of poetry, he said that in a hundred years or more surgeons would remove the heart, and "Insert a machine for the blood's circulation, that will run without losing a single pulsation." He suggested that we "will read a man's mind as we now read a book" and "diagnose cases by scanning the mind." In that far future date doctors would avoid traveling in bad weather because "by means of a network of telephone wire, we'll study each case as we sit by the fire." In his vision of the future Naylor also predicted that we will "generate babes in a new-fangled way," able to choose boy or girl, blond or brunette. He predicted that doctors would have a sure way of collecting their bills: "Some ready, exact, and infallible plan that will make a rogue act out the part of a man." Today his astoundingly accurate predictions and the humor of the poem can be appreciated by an entirely new generation.[78]

One critic of Naylor's poetry called him a "versifier," intending it to be a disparaging term.[79] Naylor's ability to compose a verse apropos of any given situation on a moment's notice was well known and, as might be expected, such verses often would not withstand critical analysis. They did, however, illustrate his quick wit and keen sense of humor. Naylor embraced the term, later using it in a phrase in an advertisement for his entertainments, "versatile genius, genial versifier; entertaining novelist, novel entertainer."[80]

Family and friends commented that many times Naylor responded to a question from a child or to a comment from his cronies at the barbershop with a catchy bit of verse. Family scrapbooks contain many interesting verses that were obviously the author's reply to various inquiries and situations. In one instance, Mildred Stephenson, a young lady from Australia, wrote to him requesting his autograph. He sent it at the bottom of a delightful (and lengthy) poem penned especially for her.

> If I remember,
> When we have June you have December;
> In other words, 'tis winter there
> When we have summer bright and fair.
> So now, perhaps, while we are roasting

In summer's heat, you may be "coasting;"
(A vagrant guess! More like, the word
That names the sport, you've never heard.
If so, it is a burning shame;
But then, my dear, you're not to blame.)
Or, clad in garments warm and nice,
Are you skimming o'er the crystal ice.
(You *do* have ice—this fact I know;
My cyclopedia tells me so)
Heighho! I've drifted quite away
From what I really meant to say.
'Twas this: I'm please—therefore, this smile!—
To think you deemed it worth your while
To send a letter o'er the sea,
To Yankeeland, a begging me
To send to you—there, there, don't laugh!
My wretched, scrawly autograph.
(My dear, it wouldn't bring a peck
Of gold, if scribbled on a check!)
But here it is; and may it please
The gods of Antipodes
To bear it far o'er sea and land
And place it safely in your hand.
    P.S.
Fair stranger, pardon this poor verse;
I *can't* write better—*can* write worse.
All anger, therefore, promptly quell –
And thank your stars I've done so well![81]

On another occasion just after the Muskingum River had flooded the area, he responded to a request from an autograph collector from Massachusetts with the following verse:

    The flood has come, the flood has gone—
    Of worldly gear we are bereft;
    But still I send my autograph—

Theresa Marie Flaherty

> The only one that I have left.
> And since the flood has come and gone—
> And left our town a sorry wreck,
> I'd like to get your autograph—
>   Appended to a goodly check.

Although he had not received a reply, he was sure a check would be forthcoming. In fact he added, "If there are others who would like to exchange autographs with me, on the same delectable terms—well, I'm open for business."[82]

Naylor enjoyed reciting his poems for Villa at home and for the children as they grew, and he welcomed their comments and suggestions. Gradually, friends, neighbors and others in his extended family gathered at his home for informal entertainments. Before long, he was presenting his material before various groups. His reputation grew locally, then throughout the state and beyond. He received complimentary notices from editors and writers from all parts of the country. Long before the first of his novels appeared in print, his poems struck a chord with everyday people.

By 1896, he was ready once again to publish a volume of collected verse. He chose seventy poems dealing with simple, commonplace incidents of everyday life and included them in a beautiful 189-page volume, *Golden Rod and Thistle Down*. Only five of the poems appeared in his first volume, *Current Coins*.[83] Although printed by Hann and Adair, the same Columbus firm that did *Current Coins*, few details are available about the financing arrangements. A. A. Coulson again provided at least some of the money for its publication. With a growing young family, Naylor's financial situation undoubtedly had not improved since his last effort. The author, evidently now more cautious, had the volume printed as an author's edition, limited to two hundred copies.[84] But for the second time, Naylor was frustrated and disappointed to find that, despite flattering reviews, poetry did not sell well.

Although he began by writing poetry exclusively, by 1896 he started writing short stories that appeared in the western dailies and news syndicates.[85] Of nearly thirty known short stories, fourteen were written under his pen name, indicating that they appeared before the turn of the twentieth century when he abandoned its use in favor of his full name.[86]

On the long, solitary rides to his patients, he worked out details of plots and characters; but it was at home, after the day's work was done, that he actually wrote. After returning to his office and seeing the last patient there, he wrote by hand on a pad of yellow paper balanced on his knee, illuminated by the lamp on his desk. Villa often sat across from him at the desk, copying each corrected and almost illegible page for the printer. He usually worked past midnight, recording the episodes that occupied his imagination on his ride that day.

It is not surprising that many of his early short stories were about doctors and medicine. He wrote about what he knew, and these stories reveal much of the man himself. In these stories, he struggled with the elements of story construction and characterizations, but his imagination flowed. Newspapers were hungry for material and did little editing prior to printing. Readers devoured everything that appeared. The only feedback he got, until his children were older, was from his wife and from comments made by his readers.

One of his first stories, "The Story of a Skeleton" is a macabre tale of a skeleton given to a young American doctor by a French colleague. The skeleton comes to life and tells the young doctor his story of dissipation and moral depravity. Before returning to the cabinet where he is kept, the skeleton leaves a cigar, one that he had picked up and chewed on, in an ashtray on a nearby table. Later, when the doctor awakens, thinking he dreamed the whole event, he finds the cigar with the teeth marks made by the skeleton. No doubt Naylor was just one of many doctors who as medical students pondered the stories behind the skeletons they handled. Naylor took it a step further and created at least one story for a skeleton.

During the early years of his medical practice, Naylor faced stiff competition from older physicians. Younger doctors seeking to establish in Malta provided another problem. His story "Two Consultations at Mam Sterling's" illustrates different approaches to the treatment of one patient. Ninety-year-old Mam Sterling is on her deathbed when two doctors are called in for consultation. Her own physician, an old man out of touch with the profession, had prescribed for her without any improvement in her condition.

Theresa Marie Flaherty

A younger consultant diagnoses everything conceivably wrong with her, while another colleague insists she is dying of old age and nothing can be done. Afterward the relatives engage in a heated discussion in an effort to determine which physician provided the correct diagnosis. The final assessment is left to the reader.

More than a hundred years before "CSI" became popular, Naylor recognized the fascination of the uninitiated in matters of medicine. Medical details play a large part in "The Coming of Sawlus," a longer story with much improved characterizations. Sawlus, an evangelist, arrives in town at the same time as a man of questionable character. When the revival begins, Hugh Connors, the druggist, expresses open hostility to the preacher. Connors' attitude alienates Amy Stanwood, his sweetheart. As a result, she befriends Sawlus, who deceives her and the rest of the congregation. With his accomplice, Sawlus robs and murders Amy's father, skillfully pointing an accusing finger at her brother, Jim, who had argued with Colonel Stanwood. The evidence seems to confirm his guilt, but Connors draws on his knowledge of medicine to use the evidence of rigor mortis, blood coagulation, and the size of the knife wound to point to the real killer.

In "The Blackmer Affair," a more complicated murder story, the medical knowledge depicted in it is also used to find a killer. Lucretia Chadwick, an assistant in the office of Blackmer and Son, falls in love with Robert, the younger Blackmer; but he is not attracted by her personality or beauty. Spurned, Lucretia, turns her charms on Robert's father who readily succumbs and proposes marriage. She accepts and, once installed as mistress of the house, again turns her attention to Robert and is once more rebuffed. Later, Robert finds his father dead, and a note pointing to suicide makes plain to those who knew the family that uncontrollable jealousy had been the cause. Doctor Will Crenshaw, Robert's cousin, arrives soon after the body is discovered and is disturbed by evidence that does not support the claim of suicide. With the assistance of another physician, and their knowledge of medicine, the baffling mystery is solved, and the true identity of the killer is established.

Minor episodes from Naylor's own past are clearly recognizable in many of his short stories, and in almost every instance a strong and admirable doctor appears as a major character. In other instances, minor characters are placed in a position of trust and authority.

In "The Stuff of Which Doctors Are Made," Naylor again draws on his own background in depicting both main characters. Young Tom comes from a poverty-stricken environment much like Naylor's. The local doctor, who takes an interest in the boy's future, is as caring as Naylor saw himself to be. When the doctor presents a once-in-a-lifetime opportunity to send the boy to medical school, Tom declines regretfully because of a promise he made to his mother. The moral stamina it takes for Tom to follow through on his promise touches the kindly physician, and Tom eventually is rewarded with the opportunity anyway.

"Wild Tom," one of the author's most delightful stories, is a heartwarming tale of a friendship between a crusty railroad engineer and a youngster who brings meaning into his life. Wild Tom, the engineer, first encounters the "Little Feller" on his regular run near Malconta,[87] where the boy in tattered clothing gathers lumps of coal along the railroad tracks. Tom sees him and yells at him to stop stealing the coal. To enforce the command, he hurls several lumps of coal at the fleeing boy. After the train passes, the lad adds these precious lumps to those in his basket. This scene is enacted daily, with the lumps of coal growing larger and larger, until the youngster fails to appear for several days. Tom searches for his young friend and, finding him ill, sends for a doctor and provides help for the needy family.[88]

Naylor learned basic grammar and English in school, but it was by actually writing that he honed those skills. His first ventures into fiction writing were well received. Encouraged, he continued flexing his imagination.

Theresa Marie Flaherty

4

Pleasures and Passions

The two decades at the turn of the twentieth century, from 1890 through the end of 1909, were the most productive in all areas of Naylor's life. His family expanded to include six children; he published the bulk of his work, both poetry and fiction; he was actively engaged in politics; and he frequently spoke and entertained, all the while maintaining his medical practice. As he stretched his imagination and explored his creativity, he became increasingly well known throughout Ohio and far beyond.

By the end of 1895, Naylor had "a hand full of babies—four little queens."[89] Olive was six years old and Lucile was four. The third daughter, Annie Budee, born on December 21, 1893, shortly after *Current Coins* appeared, was two years old. Lena Ervilla, born October 25, 1895, was a baby.

Villa sought to maintain a tranquil atmosphere for her husband when he was in his office next door, not an easy task with lively little girls. They were not allowed to bother him, but he welcomed an occasional interruption. Often, when one or another of the girls crept into his office while he was writing, it became a special moment captured in a tender-hearted poem, as in "Blue Eyes are Peeping at Me."

> I'm at work in my study—I hear a soft sound,
> And the door on its hinges swings wide;

I cease from my labor and, turning around,
   Find a wee bonny form at my side.
A sweet childish face is uplifted to mine,
   A small hand caresses my knee;
And from under brown tresses, silken and fine,
   Two blue eyes are peeping at me.[90]

Their home was Villa's domain, and looking after her husband and family was a joy to her. Lucile recalled those busy days. "Every morning, it seemed, she'd press his trousers. They just had to have a knife-edged crease. And when he'd come in from making night calls, she'd always be up to get him a bite to eat; and if he'd had a long country trip, she'd put the feed down for the horse."[91]

When Naylor came home at the end of his day, Villa admonished the children, "It's time for Papa now. Pick up your playthings and quiet down. He'll be tired." To one of the girls she said, "You get his slippers and robe." To another, "and you put his chair there by the fire."[92]

Those pleasurable moments spent with his children were transposed into a touching poem, "The Pixy Band," a poem that delightfully conveys the enchantment he no doubt looked forward to at the end of the day.

    When I forsake the busy street
       And trail my footprints home at night,
    A band of naughty pixies meet
       Me on the steps, with keen delight;
    They nimbly steal my hat, and take
       Away my overcoat and cane,
    My wet umbrella seize, and shake
       Down my back the drops of rain!
    In vain I plead: "Ah! Leave me—go,
    Why will ye clog my footsteps so—
       Why will ye hang about my knees?"
    They bend me down and mount my back,
       And heedless quite of bump or fall
    They make the floor a racing track,
       And speed me through the entrance hall.

Theresa Marie Flaherty

We reach the parlor; there they place
    For me the easy-cushioned chair,
And pull my beard and pinch my face
    And comb awry my scanty hair.
They call me "papa"—man alive!
    Sure fortune smites with heavy hand,
When I, a youth of thirty-five,
    Am father to a pixy band!
        L'envoy
Beside a row of drowsy heads,
    With moistened eyes each night I stand;
And bend and kiss them in their beds—
    God bless my little pixy band.[93]

    The Naylor's first and only son, James Robert, was born on December 27, 1897. He was still a baby in 1898, when the first spring thaw brought disastrous flooding to the Muskingum Valley. The Coulson Building, located a few blocks from the river, was quickly inundated. As water swirled through the streets, boats were rowed from building to building rescuing people trapped inside. When one reached the Naylor's

Figure 4.1 - Malta Street in Flood of 1898. Courtesy of *The Morgan County Herald.*

upstairs apartment, the four little girls clambered aboard. Frightened by the rushing water, they clung tearfully to one another as their mother gently handed three-month-old Robert to the rescuers before climbing into the rocking boat. Cradled once again in his mother's arms, the tiny baby slept through it all, unaware of the disastrous events taking place on his adventure outside the warmth and safety of his home.

Figure 4.2 - Malta Street. Courtesy of *The Morgan County Herald.*

The family's next move was into a house built in Malta in 1888 for Villa's mother, Mrs. Walker, who was no longer able to maintain such a large place. She moved into a home nearby, an arrangement that worked out well for both households. Affectionately dubbed "Elmhurst," the family's home was a magnificent, red brick, two-story house with thirteen rooms. A large front porch curved around one side, and ornate shingles covered the second story. Standing high above a brick-paved street, the house faced a beautiful view of the river with the city of McConnelsville and a background of hills beyond. Visitors climbed twenty-seven steps in two tiers from the street to the front porch.

The grounds around the house consisted of five or six acres, two lots wide, including the hillside behind the house, down a hollow and up to the crest of the ridge. Wild flowers filled the lawn in summer and ran riot into the woods sloping steeply upward away from the house. Bird feeders on the big elms attracted many different species, and hummingbirds nesting nearby feasted on the nectar of the honeysuckle near the front porch. A wooden barn built on the first rise in back of the house accommodated two horses and a buggy used by Naylor in visiting his widely scattered clientele.

Figure 4.3 - *Elmhurst*, the Naylor Family Home. Courtesy of Greg and Ellen Hill.

At the age of 42, Naylor thought his family complete. Olive was a teenager of fourteen, and Robert was five years old when Bonnie Jean, the last child, arrived on July 4, 1903. Like her sister Lucile, Jean was teased for keeping her father at home on another important day, for he often gave a patriotic speech at Fourth of July celebrations.

By this time Naylor had already moved his office from the space above Coulson's store to a two-room space over the bank in Malta. The large front room served as both his reception area and his office. One of the two rocking chairs was for his patients, the other for himself. In the back room he treated the patients who came to him. A large cabinet held the different compotes that he used in mixing his own medicines.

Nearly six feet tall, Naylor was a slender, long-legged man with clear, keen, blue eyes that gazed steadfastly through wire-rimmed spectacles. The full beard he wore for many years was thick and dark. The iron-gray hair at his temples gave him a distinguished appearance that was often at odds with his temperament, for when his good humor erupted, he seemed hardly more than a boy. Someone who knew him well said, "He has an air of brusqueness sometimes, but, huh! Who's afraid? We know the man under the manner."[94] Villa shared his fine sense of humor, and their antics caused much merriment in the family. Ben Fouts, a distant relative and neighbor, was especially appreciative of their sense of humor and became the subject of a witty couplet written by Naylor for his girls to tease their mother:

    To Mine Girlies
    Your Mom and I
        Are at the Outs;
    The trouble's all
        About Ben Fouts.
            - Daddie.[95]

Figure 4.4 - Naylor's Upstairs Office in Malta. Courtesy of Rick Shriver, McConnelsville, Ohio.

Theresa Marie Flaherty

Fouts always waved as he passed the Naylor girls or their mother at the window or on the porch, and they waved back. If Naylor was around, however, Ben would ignore the doctor, pretending he had just been caught in a daring act as he ducked behind a bit of shrubbery that barely concealed him. Naylor would explode with laughter, joined by Fouts and the family.

Although not closely related, Villa was a Naylor who married a Naylor, and several times when she and the children were out walking, someone would look at the girls, point to one and say, "Oh, I think this one looks more like the Naylors." Villa always agreed emphatically, but a smile danced in her eyes, and the girls, looking on, struggled to suppress giggles.[96]

The family loved spending time together outdoors. They often picnicked below the dam in Malta, where the girls waded in the water and Robert swam. On long Sunday walks, the whole family tramped along Doudna run, a lovely stretch of wooded, hilly country just a short distance south of Malta. Naylor instilled in his children a love of nature and taught them the names of plants and the birds found in the area. He loved to catch a bumblebee in a hollyhock blossom by closing the petals over the bee. Then he held the blossoms to each of the children's ears so they could hear the bee's noisy complaint.[97] According to his children, he "could imitate the sounds of a bee to perfection, from the moment he was trapped, until he was released and went zooming on his busy way."[98]

At night, they would walk outdoors and look up at the sky above. Villa, who knew some astronomy, would point out the constellations. "Never would I have known Casiopeia, Andromeda, Orion, Bootes,

Figure 4.5 - Mrs. Naylor in 1913.
Courtesy of Jean Naylor Finley.

or even the big and little dippers, —any of them, in fact—but for Mom," said Lucile.⁹⁹

Recalling those happy days, Naylor often laughed, telling the children how he had "educated them in the higher branches."⁵ In the midst of a thunderstorm, he gathered the family close around him on the porch at Elmhurst. Together they watched lightning streak across the sky and listened to the rain beating fiercely against the house. The children learned to enjoy the rumble of thunder and not be afraid of it.

The only boy in houseful of girls, Robert was a daily reminder to his father of his own boyhood. Robert said, "When we boys used to get into devilment, the others would say: 'Don't let our dads find out about this.' But that was the first thing I would do: Tell Dad. And would he give me thunder! But he'd help me get out of the trouble, and then I wouldn't do it again."¹⁰⁰

Naylor was an avid photographer and often brought along his camera. An early biographic sketch reported, "He is an enthusiastic, amateur photographer, and wastes his substance in the riotous exposure of dry plates. With his camera and the companionship of his dog, he loved to wander up and down the green valley, drinking in the beauties of the rural scenery."¹⁰¹ Naylor admitted, "I wreck my credit upon pictures, and

Figure 4.6 - Naylor Outdoors. Courtesy of Jean Naylor Finley.

bankrupt myself buying books. Mrs. Naylor threatens to move out and leave me, in full and lone possession of my treasured trash."[102]

The Naylors were a tightly knit family and considered a bit eccentric by some of their neighbors. They provided their own entertainment, usually family gatherings, but occasional guests were invited to join them. Group parties with schoolmates enlivened the house without much planning, and in the evenings the family played dominos or other board games. For a long time Villa, because of her religious background, was opposed to having any playing cards in the house, but eventually they enjoyed playing casino, seven-up, and Flinch.

Naylor's view of religion was rather unorthodox. Sometimes mistakenly thought of as an atheist or agnostic, he was neither; he called himself "a fixed scientist and a rationalist."[103] His views evolved gradually over the years, but the one person to have the greatest influence on them was undoubtedly Gatewood. Gatewood did not accept the church's beliefs and called them absurd and unscientific. During the years of his

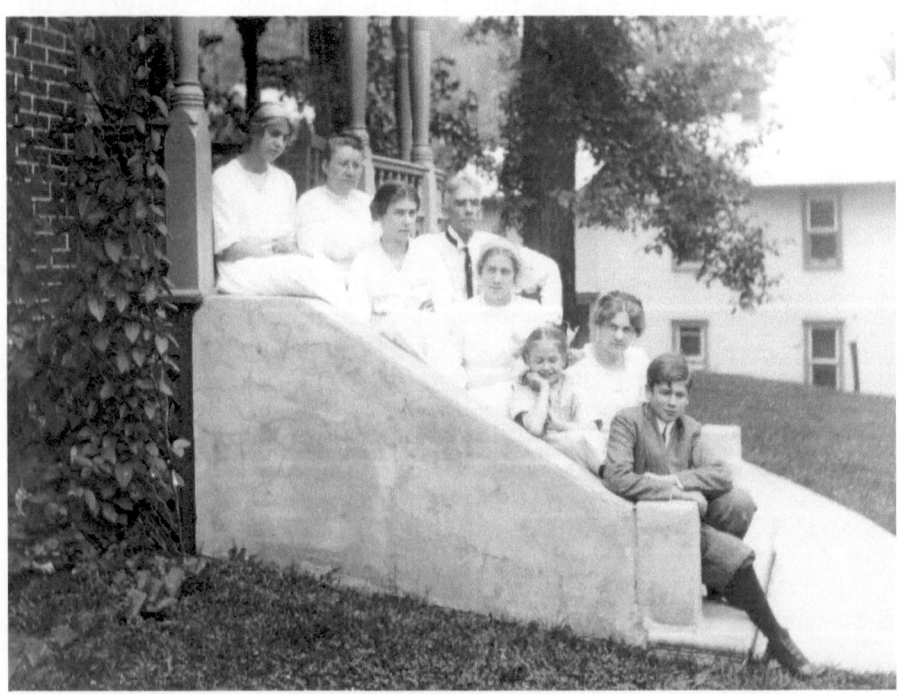

Figure 4.7 - Naylor Family, 1913: Anne, Mrs. Naylor, Lucile, Dr. Naylor, Lena, Jean, Olive, and Robert. Courtesy of Jean Naylor Finley.

apprenticeship, Naylor learned a great deal more than medicine from this severely independent man, and he readily adopted many of Gatewood's views.

Although critical of churches when he married Villa, a Methodist, he often attended church, and the children were brought up in the church and participated in many programs. Naylor believed that a lot of good was done by the church for people who needed it, but he was not one of those who needed it. "You can't talk religion to me because I don't understand your terms," Naylor once said as he stood gazing at autumn colors blazing on a hillside, "But when I see the color and beauty of that hillside I realize there is an intelligence beyond our own in which we can trust."[104]

Theresa Marie Flaherty

5
Serialized and Historical Fiction

Perhaps because poetry was not the profitable endeavor that he hoped for, Naylor began writing longer stories. More likely, he recognized an opportunity that evolved in 1836 when Charles Dickens, then a young reporter for London's *Morning Chronicle*, published the first serialized story.[105] Newspapers discovered that by publishing several serialized stories staggered over the course of several weeks they could attract and retain more readers. Before one serialized story finished, another began, thus ensuring that readers would keep coming back.

Naylor's earliest known serial, "Beggars Awheel," was written for boys and appeared in *The Ohio Farmer* in eight chapters in a section for "Young Folks" from December 3, 1896, through January 21, 1897. In characterizing boys, Naylor drew on experiences from his own boyhood, vividly presenting childhood emotions that held the reader's attention. The adventure story, about two teenage boys on a 250-mile bicycle trip, was written at a time when bicycles were considered strange contraptions. In their travel, the city-bred boys journey through the picturesque Ohio countryside where Naylor grew up. To the country people they encounter, the bicycle is a peculiar mode of transportation, and an expensive one at that, hardly the type two penniless boys would have. Yet, with the loss of all their money, they must resort to accepting handouts. The rustic characters they meet along the way add much to the drama, and Naylor's use of dialect enhanced the characterization. The boys are fascinated with threshing operations on a farm and with water-powered mills, the sweet memories of Naylor's own childhood. There is no obvious moralizing in the story, and it is quite entertaining. For today's readers, it provides an interesting contrast to the present.

Another story for boys copyrighted in 1897 was "Ben's Adventure." In this story, young Ben and his father discover a hollow log in the woods near their home when they are out hunting. Later it becomes a refuge for Ben when he encounters a mother bear and her cub. Unable to reach Ben from either end, the bear tears at the log and sends it rolling down a steep incline where Ben is trapped when it hits bottom. His dog finds him and he is rescued. Naylor knew every inch of Newton Ridge as a boy, and this story reflects those memories, as do many passages in Naylor's body of work.

One of the best of Naylor's early stories, "A Spike from the Underground Railroad," is based on a true incident, and apparently it was his first venture into historical fiction. Written barely more than thirty years after the end of the Civil War, the story is set in "Kikertown," easily recognized as Pennsville, a strongly abolitionist village that figured prominently in the "underground railroad."[106] This was a network of escape routes stretching from the southern states into the north and on up to Canada, and described using railroad terminology. Fugitive slaves reaching Pennsville were not likely to be captured because they were moved quickly to safety. The runaway slaves fleeing the South were referred to as the "passengers," and the "conductors" were the guides who led them from one "station" to the next. The runaways traveled at night, remaining hidden in safe-houses, barns, haylofts, etc., during the day. Naylor's story describes a cleverly conceived plan. Quakers distract slave owners on the trail of three blacks, thus giving others time to move them to the next station. By the time the owners realize what has happened, the slaves are long gone.

From another historical episode associated with the Civil War in Morgan County, Naylor developed an interesting story, "One of Morgan's Men," about a man under the command of the Confederate guerilla commander, General John Hunt Morgan, on a raid through Ohio. In Naylor's fictional account, the general and his men cross the Muskingum River at Eagleport, above McConnelsville, and near this point the man is badly injured. The local doctor recognizes the Confederate soldier as a southerner but keeps his identity a secret because of the anti-southern feelings of the Prinston home where the young man is given asylum. In the love story that follows, the daughter is torn between loyalty to her family and her feelings for the stranger.

"Jud Trainor's Ghost" is another short story set during the Civil War, but it is not based on a historical episode per se. Jud, an ungainly young man, manages to snare the village belle for a bride. For Dessie, it was a happy marriage, and she bore him a daughter. Jud, however, was insanely jealous of any man who even looked at his wife. When the Civil War breaks out, he sold his farm, gave her money to live on while he was gone, and carefully hid the rest. By the end of the war, when he did not return, she was in desperate circumstances, forced to work for neighboring farmers' wives to support herself and her child, just as Naylor's own mother had. Eventually Dessie marries again and, despite hardships that fill her life, she is happy—until the day Jud Trainor's ghost appears. Jud had told her he would haunt her if she ever married again. Others in the village see Jud's ghost and the country buzzes with speculation. Some claim that it is Jud's ghost; others say that Jud himself has returned. Finally, with the help of the village doctor, Dessie learns that Jud's purpose is to lead her to the buried money that now belongs to her.

With a number of serialized stories already published in newspapers and these early ventures into historical fiction that buoyed his confidence, he tackled a broader area in the history of Ohio, one he found in his own backyard. Naylor began writing what eventually became a trilogy of historical novels. Each of the stories was published serially in the *Ohio State Journal* prior to its appearance in book form, but in a different order than the publication of the books. Reviewers of the books in the trilogy most likely were not aware of their prior appearance in the *State Journal*. Based on the actual order in which the stories were written, Naylor's growth as a writer is obvious and quite different than an analysis based on the order of publication in hardback.

Each of the stories was accompanied by illustrations done by Harry J. Westerman, a cartoonist for the *Ohio State Journal*. Naylor and Westerman worked together on many other occasions and the two became good friends, as did their families.

Naylor exercised great care in verifying the material in each of the stories, all woven around true incidents in Ohio history. He searched contemporary records for information to accurately describe every battle, every army, and every historical person. Naylor claimed that he never had a critic find a single historical misstatement in his historical novels. "Every battle, every army, every historical person is described accurately from contemporary records. You can't believe how much trouble I took to find out how Mad Anthony looked. I wanted to know the color of his hair and eyes. How did he talk and act? I finally found what I wanted in a rare pamphlet."[107]

Figure 5.1 - Naylor with Harry Westerman.
Courtesy of Jean Naylor Finley

In the Days of St. Clair

Naylor was best known to readers of the *Ohio State Journal* as S. Q. Lapius, from his frequent contributions of poetry and fiction. With the serialization of his historical novels, he added the signature Dr. J. B. Naylor. Each serialization was preceded by an announcement in the *Journal*. "In the Days of St. Clair" was the first. The announcement appeared the week before the first installment and included "Interesting Facts about a Rising Young Ohio Author and His Latest and Most Powerful Work."[108] The editor commented on the fact that few contemporary writers came from or wrote about Ohio despite the varied elements of population and picturesque scenery. He was pleased with his discovery and optimistic about Naylor's future as a writer.

> The State Journal takes pleasure this morning in announcing the early and exclusive publication of a splendidly written and exceedingly interesting novel by a new Ohio author. The exclusive rights have been purchased by the State Journal and it will not appear in any other newspaper or in book form until its publication in the Sunday Journal is concluded![109]

In the Days of St. Clair appeared in the Sunday issues beginning on December 5, 1897, through February 27, 1898. It covers an exciting episode in the early history of the first settlement and describes the 1791 massacre of settlers at Big Bottom along the Muskingum River in Morgan County. The Big Bottom massacre occurred only a few miles from Pennsville where the author was born and quite close to Stockport where he worked as a young man. This tragic event was often a topic of discussion, and Naylor was constantly reminded of it on his frequent trips through the area to visit his patients.

The opening chapters are laid in the Shenandoah Valley of West Virginia, but the characters move to the Ohio wilderness after the settlement is established at Marietta. The settlement was running smoothly when Naylor's fictional character, Paul Graydon, arrived, although the Indians were growing more restless as pioneers extended the colonization. Despite occasional harassment by the redskins, the settlers felt secure with two strong stockades not far away, Campus Martius at Marietta and Fort Harmer on the opposite side of the river.

Fictional events leading to the massacre are cleverly woven into the tapestry of actual occurrences. Graydon joins a group of settlers forming a colony at Big Bottom, thirty-six miles up the

Muskingum River from Marietta where they erected a blockhouse and two cabins, but he was absent on the fateful night. The settlers, knowing that the Indians seldom went on the warpath in winter, became careless of possible danger. Twelve settlers were brutally murdered and five captured. Marie Fontanelle is a fictional sixth captive added by the author. Graydon and a Shawnee friend pursue the Indians to their village to rescue Marie.

Under Mad Anthony's Banner

General Anthony Wayne's brilliant campaign in 1795 provided the background for Naylor's second narrative, "Under Mad Anthony's Banner." The serialization of this story was also preceded by a lengthy announcement in the Journal. The article said:

> The author has surpassed his former effort and has produced a novel that will rank as one of the most brilliant and intensely interesting historical stories of the year....We have no hesitancy in saying after a careful reading of the manuscript that 'Under Mad Anthony's Banner' will immediately take rank as the finest historical novel dealing with life in the Western wilds nearly 100 years ago that has been written in recent years.[110]

Besides General Wayne, Naylor used two figures from real life as characters in the story, Lewis Wetzel, a famous scout and backwoodsman, and Simon Girty, a notorious outlaw. The story centers on Hal Barton, an Americanized Englishman whose wife has disappeared. Befriended by Wetzel, Barton enrolls as a scout with Wetzel under Wayne and participates in his campaign. Barton discovers that his wife has been captured by the Indians and that his British cousin and longtime rival is involved. Barton later rescues a young woman, Judith Sterling, from the unwanted attentions of a young officer. In a daring plot twist Naylor has Barton fall in love with her while yet married to someone else. Barton learns that the officer is General Wayne's aide and discovers that he is a traitor in league with

Girty. Barton obtains proof that will convince the general of his aide's treachery, finds his wife, and resolves his personal problems.

Following its serialization from November 27, 1898, to March 5, 1899, the *Journal* decided to publish *Under Mad Anthony's Banner* in hardback. This edition of the book was copyrighted 1899.

The Sign of the Prophet

The last of the trilogy, "The Sign of the Prophet," appeared in the *Journal's* Sunday issues from October 28, 1900, to February 10, 1901. In announcing the serialization of the last of the trilogy, the Columbus State Journal said:

> Dr. Naylor's previous stories of early Ohio life have been so greatly enjoyed by the thousands of readers of The Ohio State Journal, that a lengthy description of his new work is not necessary. It is enough to say that "The Sign of the Prophet" is by far the strongest, most absorbing, and best work which this rising Ohio author has done, surpassing in intense and sustained interest both "In the Days of St. Clair" and "Under Mad Anthony's Banner."[111]

This story depicts events connected with the battle of Tippecanoe, where General William Henry Harrison faced a force of Indians from various tribes in the Northwest Territory. Because Tecumseh, their leader, was absent at the time of the battle, his brother, Tenskwatawa, the Prophet, assumed authority. Tecumseh, by forming a confederacy with southern tribes, hoped to force the Americans from the Mississippi and Ohio Valleys. Before the battle, a council was held at Vincennes, the capital of the Northwest Territory. General John Gibson, Secretary of the Territory, discovered a plot to assassinate Harrison, who was serving as governor. Convinced that war was inevitable, Harrison assembled an army consisting of a detachment of United States troops and militia from Kentucky and Indiana.

Ross Douglass, Naylor's fictional hero, joins Harrison's army as a scout and is wounded and captured at Tippecanoe. La Violette, a white captive adopted by the Prophet as his daughter, nurses him back to health. When Douglass returns home, he discovers his sweetheart was captured in his absence. When he finds her, she is married to a cruel and vicious man. Douglass secures the talisman of the Prophet, drives the Indians back from Fort Miami, and claims the beautiful La Violette for his bride.

The Trilogy

There are commonalities across the three books that reflect Naylor's style. His determination to adhere to historical accuracy sometimes weakened the narratives, but his clever use of real episodes compensated for a lack of originality. "The Sign of the Prophet" is the best of Naylor's historical narratives and reflects his effort to improve his style of writing.

The framework for each of the stories is quite similar, and many comparisons can be made between the sets of characters of each. There is a hero, a love interest, another woman, a villain, the hero's companion, and a minor character in each story who share similar traits. Graydon, Barton, and Douglass are the typical heroes, and they make their entry into the story under similar circumstances. Marie Fontanelle, Judith Sterling, and La Violette, the love interests, are portrayed in a similar fashion. Each is beautiful and involved in a romantic triangle. Hester Lovelace, Margaret Barton, and Amy Larkin are the other women involved with the heroes. Of the villains, Red Wallace, Simon Girty, and George Hilliard, only Girty is an authentic historical character. Silverheels, Wetzel, and Bright Wing, companions to the heroes, provide Naylor with an opportunity to portray the white man's attitude toward the Indians. Gumbo, Rory McFarlan, and Joe Farley are minor characters who play comparable roles in each story by adding humor with their use of dialect. All three stories have a similar surprising ending. In each story, the identity of an important individual is revealed and proves to be related to a main character.

Although Naylor used a formula in constructing each of these stories, his growth as a writer is evident in how he handles his characters. His growth is most evident in how he handles the female characters from one story to the next. He was straightforward in handling the female characters in "In the Days of St. Clair." Marie Fontanelle is obviously the heroine and Hester Lovelace is clearly the opposite. Suspense is added in "Under Mad Anthony's Banner" because the differences between Judith Sterling and Margaret Barton are not so clearly defined. Since Margaret is the hero's wife, the reader is led to assume that she will emerge as the heroine. Instead Judith is introduced as a new love interest. Although Hal Barton remains true to his wife until her death, the story is undermined. Naylor avoids this pitfall in "The Sign of the Prophet" when Amy Larkin loses Douglass' love through her own actions, and La Violette emerges as the heroine.

Naylor's vivid description of life on the frontier, enhanced by his intimate knowledge of the area and his sense of history, convey the atmosphere of the time. Young audiences and those familiar with the places and events no doubt enjoyed the colorful tales despite some improbable twists in plot, the unlikely coincidences, and chance meetings, as well as the much too similar plot line in all three stories.

By the time he completed the entire trilogy in 1900, Naylor's health was becoming more and more troublesome. His early practice of medicine with the necessity of visiting patients by buggy or on horseback affected him seriously. In recalling the effort of writing his novels, he said, "I lost five to ten pounds every time I wrote a novel. Usually I wrote one in four to five months and I always had nervous indigestion when I finished. The characters give their creator no rest. They were the most restless bedfellows I ever had, those characters. They woke you up in the night and put you to work."[112]

6
Success as a Novelist

Once the first episode of "The Sign of the Prophet" made its appearance in the *Ohio State Journal* in October, 1900, Naylor wasted no time in tackling his next project. The subject for his next one was far more personal. He wrote about himself, disguised in the figure of a man he called Ralph Marlowe. He wrote about the inhabitants of a remote village that he named Babylon, describing and capturing their character traits because he knew them so well.

Figure 6.1 - Stockport Street in Front of Gatewood's Drug Store.

Naylor added interest to the story with his descriptions of the country village, general store, neighborly gossip, and people in their natural surroundings. Naylor was a keen observer of those with whom he had frequent contact, and he enjoyed listening to their anecdotes. They were the inspiration for the characters of the rural community that made *Ralph Marlowe* such a success. Besides himself, the author identified three characters as real individuals: Dr, Gatewood as Dr. Barwood; Ernest B. Schneider of Zanesville, who was depicted as Leonidas Walingford Crider, the breezy drummer; and John Brooks of Stockport who was portrayed as Jep Tucker, Dr. Barwood's hired man.

Ralph Marlowe is a stranger when he arrives in Babylon and accepts a position as a drug clerk in the office of Dr. Barwood, an eccentric, misunderstood physician. Despite warnings that no man has been able to work very long with the doctor, Marlowe remains. He begins by thoroughly cleaning the drug store, revamping the merchandise, rearranging the shelf-ware, over-hauling contents of drawers and showcases, and placing fresh goods and advertising matter in the windows. Barwood gives no indication of approval when he returns. Instead, he drops his muddy saddlebags and coat on the clean counter. Marlowe politely tells the doctor he will hang his things in the entrance to the basement.

"No," Barwood answers. "Leave them where they are." Marlowe insists they are in his way, but the doctor is adamant. "I can't help that. Leave them alone. I want them handy."

Calmly but firmly, Marlowe picks up the offending items and carries them from the room, saying, "I'll get them for you when you want them, Doctor."[113]

Expecting a storm from the fiery Dr. Barwood, an observer is startled to see a flicker of a smile as the doctor turns on his heel to leave.

A series of similar incidents reveal both men's personalities. Marlowe concedes graciously to the doctor's demands, but expects no interference in fulfilling them. By maintaining his independence and dignity under the most trying circumstances, the apprentice earns the older man's friendship.

JAMES BALL NAYLOR

Marlowe was hardworking, resourceful, and independent with no weaknesses to mar his character, except for an inflexibility that proves to be an asset. Marlowe uses his influence without being offensive and works toward a moral regeneration of the village. Lon Crider, the drummer; the lazy, worthless Jim Crawford; Morris McDivitt, ruined at the gambling tables and saved by Barwood's religious daughter, are personalities that command the attention of the reader.

Marlowe falls in love with one of Barwood's daughters, but she suspects that he is concealing his past after reading a letter that could be easily misinterpreted. Eventually, the mystery is cleared up, the secret ceases to be the curse of his life, and he is free to marry the girl.

Ralph Marlowe gave Naylor more satisfaction than any other of his prose writing. When asked why he wrote it, he promptly replied:

> I wrote it because I was afflicted with "ink fever"—and must write something; I wrote it to get rid of an incubus that had been weighing me down for years—a feeling that I must write it: I wrote because I believe that one writes best of the things he knows best.... As an afterthought, I would say that I wrote "Ralph Marlowe" for the reason that it was, and is,—a part of me."[114]

While the book is fiction, in the preface Naylor described the book as "...the legitimate child of actual experience." He admitted that he was Ralph Marlowe and confirmed that many of the incidents were factual, that the characters were living personalities, and that Babylon was the village of Stockport.[115]

Naylor was a personable young man, well known to everyone in the area on friendly, relaxed terms, quite different from the atmosphere he encountered in the drug store. From the brief biographies available of his early mentor, Gatewood was all that Naylor showed Barwood to be: fiery, headstrong, brilliant, and individualistic, yet a gentleman, philosopher, and philanthropist.

In Gatewood, Naylor had found the model he would use to sculpt and hone his own persona.

Although Dr. Barwood's character was based on Gatewood, and in the story Marlowe married Barwood's daughter, Gatewood actually had no daughters. Naylor did marry the daughter of another distinguished citizen of Stockport, Captain Charles J. Gibson, a war hero and the owner of a mercantile store. His daughter, Myrta, was Naylor's first wife.

Naylor decided to send this manuscript to a publishing house. They kept it for quite some time while he waited impatiently. When the manuscript was rejected, his hopes were shattered. The dreadful condition of the returned manuscript assured him that it had been read, but the letter from the publishers abruptly stated that they were not interested. Their basic summation was that the story showed "no particular style or merit," yet they agreed it was "a sweet and readable tale of deep human interest."[116]

His disappointment was obvious, but their reaction reminded him of the first time Pud Norton, a friend of his, tried a chaw of tobacco. After chewing it awhile, he spat it out. When asked if it was good, he replied, "It was good—but I didn't like it."[117]

Believing that the novel had real value, Naylor sent the manuscript to another publisher. Once more it was rejected, but with a different evaluation. They found the story "somewhat sordid" and "wholly lacking in deep human interest but it is quite well written—in a strong individual style."[118]

The two opposing opinions, although a disappointment, did not completely extinguish Naylor's sense of humor, "the game was getting interesting," he thought. "I decided at once that the literary life was the life for me. Here were two opinions, from those in authority, diametrically opposed. It was 'pay your money and take your choice.' The one might be right, or the other—for the life of me, I didn't know; and the element of chance appealed to the gamester in me."[119]

Again and again the manuscript was sent off in the hope of finding a publisher, until at last it was accepted by the Saalfield Publishing Company of Akron, Ohio, primarily publishers of children's books. The company was founded by Arthur J. Saalfield in 1900. Saalfield moved to Akron, Ohio, in 1897 and acquired the Werner Company's publishing department. His wife, Ada Louise Sutton Saalfield, an accomplished writer and poet, was instrumental in the success of the company as she provided her husband with a constant flow of manuscripts for the Saalfield imprint.[120] No information is available concerning Naylor's contract with Saalfield or the royalties that he was to receive; but this, his most successful book, must have brought him a considerable amount of money.

In the months before it appeared, Saalfield announced to the reading public that they had "discovered a new literary light—a scintillant, dazzling literary star" and gave vague hints about the story.[121] By providing some information about the author, they hoped to keep the public dangling with expectancy until the book finally appeared.

The book gained immediate popularity following its publication in March, 1901, and for six months it was among the top six books on the *Bookman*'s list of best sellers. The author received wide acknowledgment in the literary world, and he was inundated with reviews from newspapers across the country and from England.

The public was captivated by the glimpse of contemporary rural Ohio that Naylor presented. Comparisons were made to *David Harum*, a popular novel written by Edward Westcott, published in 1898, to John Uri Lloyd's *Tales of Kentuck*, and others. Reviews of *Ralph Marlowe* and Naylor's other books provide insight into the contemporary appreciation for his ability as a writer.

Most reviewers felt the author handled the Jep Tucker character deftly. One review by William Hilton, in the *Boston Home Journal*, is typical:

> I like every bit of it. I was immensely interested in the opening chapter, when Ralph Marlowe arrives in Babylon. I like Dr. Naylor's style of description. He has just enough to give you an idea of the hour and day. And he does not have too much. I liked the "breezy travelling man for Baldy Drug Company." A better "drummer" seldom gets between covers. I wanted to know about a town that "covers half a township

and has about six hundred population?" I have known some old codgers like Jep Tucker. So he seems a friend. His similes ought to be in literature. "Slicker'n a peeled sapling," is good. So is "hangs onto a bargain like a burr to a cow's tail." Better yet is "slower than thick molasses." Who hasn't been like Jep, and "felt like a rooster in a millpon", neither ridin' n'r a-walkin'? And Jep is not the only "character" in Dr. Naylor's book. He himself says "Ol' Tom's funnier'n a funeral."[122]

Naylor belonged to clipping services in Boston and New York, and he was inundated with reviews from newspapers across the country as well as of reviews published in England and Scotland where *Ralph Marlowe* was also well received. One reviewer said, "The author has quite a Dickens-like eye for quaint character, and it is his two or three delightfully original types which make the book so interesting and amusing. The author need hardly have told us that these are people in real life, for we know them at once as real men."[123] Another said that appreciation of the "traditional American sense of humor" was less than enthusiastic and that many failed to understand the rural character depicted by Jep Tucker.[124] Jep's sense of humor not only delineates his character, but also provides the most outstanding facet of his personality.

In a London newspaper, a reviewer wrote:

> There are good things to be found in its pages, but there is also a superabundance of Yankee humour, which does not appeal to the Britisher.... There is a real human touch about the whimsical old doctor, and he lingers in the memory when Jep Tucker's sayings, which are far better than his interminable stories, have faded away.[125]

Naylor remarked in an interview that he once told John Brooks he was thinking of using him in a story, and in a characteristic manner, John replied: "You'll have an uphill job of it, in my 'pinion," his eyes sparkling humorously, "fer I've been tryin' that very thing all my life-to make myself a character. An' I ain't no nearer havin' one 'n I was w'en

I first started."[126]

Jep Tucker's tales resulted from the many hours John Brooks spent in Gatewood's drug store spinning yarns with Naylor, yarns that are honest and typical of rural America. Another reviewer said of Naylor: "He is by no means a novice, but a keen observer, and has aptly interpreted human nature as he found it in the remote village. He has made his book a bright mirror in which character traits are clearly defined, reflecting without the exaggeration which so often mars works of this sort...."[127]

No doubt Saalfield expected the book to do well, but when it became a best seller they were not prepared for its runaway success nor were they equipped to produce the large numbers of volumes necessary to meet the demand. The first edition, released in early March, 1901, consisted of a printing of 5,000 books, followed in rapid succession by three more editions of 15,000 each. The second edition was printed three weeks after the first release, followed less than a month later by the third. A fourth edition was printed again the following month. A total of 50,000 copies were printed, a large printing for that time. The Werner Company, book manufacturers in Akron, Ohio, were unable to provide sufficient copies. They printed some of the additional copies, and Saalfield contracted with the Robert Smith Printing Company in Lansing, Michigan, to supplement the production, resulting in some variation in the bindings and title pages. The book sold at retail for a dollar and a half.

The immediate success of *Ralph Marlowe* impressed many people all over the country. They wished to know more about the

Figure 6.2 - Ralph Marlowe with Book Jacket.

author, and Naylor was pressed to "tell the public over and over how he came to commit the crime, and pose for innumerable photographs." [128] At first he enjoyed the limelight. "Judging from what the critics said of it, my story was the 'great American novel," he said. "I sat up nights to read those things and slept with them under my pillow."[129]

When the novelty of success wore off, Naylor quit sitting for photographs and submitting to interviews and attempted to resume once more a "sane and sensible commonplace existence."[130] But fame had touched his life, and he would never be free of its effects—nor did he really wish to be.

Naylor's publisher, Saalfield, immediately capitalized on the success of *Ralph Marlowe* by publishing *The Sign of the Prophet,* the first book in what eventually would be considered his historical trilogy. An early review of an advanced copy of *Ralph Marlowe* appeared January 13, 1901, while "The Sign of the Prophet" was still running serially in the *Ohio State Journal.*[131] By now, Saalfield knew they had a marketable author and quickly obtained the rights to *The Sign of the Prophet*, actually the last one of the three written and the last of Naylor's historical trilogy to appear serially. The last episode appeared in *The Ohio State Journal* on February 10, 1901, barely a month before *Ralph Marlowe* appeared.

The following year, in 1902, Saalfield published the second book of the trilogy, *In the Days of St. Clair.* It was, however, the first one written. The cover of the first edition was an attractive one with a picture of General St. Clair on both it and the dust jacket.[132] A photograph of the Burroughs Book Store in Cleveland, Ohio, displaying 850 to 1,000 copies of this book in its window, confirms the extent of the author's popularity.

Naylor enjoyed his celebrity status and was always delighted to discuss his books with those who read them. On one occasion, someone took exception to a statement in *In the Days of St. Clair* and said it was impossible for Gumbo to see light in the eyes of the panther at night when there was no torch to reflect the light. Naylor was adamant and recalled that in his boyhood he had seen the eyes of cows shine in reflection of the moonlight, and he stated that was what happened in the case of the panther.[133]

Figure 6.3 - Burroughs Book Store in Cleveland, Ohio, with Naylor's 1901 novel, *In the Days of St. Clair*, displayed in the window.

In 1903 *Under Mad Anthony's Banner*, previously copyrighted by J. B. Naylor in 1899, was recopyrighted and published by Saalfield without acknowledgment of its prior appearance. This was the second story written, but it was the last of the trilogy to be published by the Akron firm. The trade edition, bound in the same uniform red and white binding as the other books, was printed by the Robert Smith Printing Company.[134] The first edition, with a distinctive red cover similar to the first two books in the trilogy, was printed by the Werner Company in Akron.

As the years passed and Naylor's popularity grew, many of his readers and critics were unaware of the serialization of Naylor's historical trilogy in the *Ohio State Journal* and assumed that the novels were written in the order of their publication by Saalfield. While each story stands on its own merits and is enjoyable to read no matter what the order, all were written before *Ralph Marlowe*, yet all were published in hardback after its appearance, altering the perception of Naylor's evolution as a writer. Because the trilogy was not published in the sequence that it was written, and the last, and the best written of the three, was published first, reviewers failed to see the improvement in Naylor's writing.

A number of novels of a similar genre appeared after Naylor's historical trilogy. Pearl Zane Grey, who was twelve years younger than Naylor, grew up in Zanesville, Ohio, less than thirty miles from Malta. Grey's first three novels are similar enough to suggest that he may have been influenced by Naylor. Additionally, both writers read many of the same collections of stories about border warfare that were then popular.

Grey's family was living in Columbus when Naylor's stories were serialized in the *Ohio State Journal*, and it seems unlikely that Naylor's works escaped his attention. If Grey did not read the serialized stories, he must have seen the hardback editions. It is quite possible that Grey received some inspiration from reading Naylor's historical novels for they were in circulation before Grey's first book, *Betty Zane*, appeared in 1903. Grey, unsuccessful in finding a publisher, printed *Betty Zane* at his own expense. *The Spirit of the Border*, written in 1904, followed *Betty Zane*. The manuscript for *The Last Trail* was completed in 1905 before he found a publisher for the former. *The Spirit of the Border* was published in 1906 and *The Last Trail* in 1909.[135] These and other of Grey's books were found in Naylor's library and were read and enjoyed by his son, Robert, as well.

A similarity in the three novels from the pen of each writer is apparent and, with some justification, both were compared with James Fenimore Cooper in their portrayal of historical episodes. Each author dealt with the same period of American history, the same general locale and, in some instances, with characters based on the same historical personages. Grey, however, had an advantage in one respect for there were members of the Zane family that he could write about with some authenticity. The famous exploit of his great aunt, Betty Zane, at Fort Henry provided the inspiration for his first book; and in the two succeeding books his grandfather,

Ebenezer, and his great uncle, Jonathan Zane, were important characters.

If Naylor influenced Grey, Grey never admitted it. Grey expanded his horizons when he moved on to write about the great west. This theme, one that fascinated a great many people, gained him immense popularity, and he capitalized on it again and again. Naylor was as competent as Grey in creating characterizations and constructing plots, but what differentiates the two men is that Naylor chose to remain in his beloved Muskingum Valley, pursuing his own wide range of interests rather than focusing on what would most interest the public.

7
Marketable Endeavors

Ralph Marlowe brought Naylor much deserved recognition, as well as a favorable impact on his financial situation, at least initially. Earnings from the book and those that followed were less than spectacular. While the family's standard of living was definitely elevated, the income he received for his novels and from his platform work was not enough to make him a wealthy man. Little is known about his personal finances or investments, but it is clear that he struggled throughout his career to find ways of profiting from his diverse talents.

During the years from 1901 through 1903 when the historical trilogy was published in hardback, Naylor was an especially busy man. He continued writing short stories during this period, and they appeared in the popular magazines of the day. These later stories are identified by the use of the author's full name. Before 1900 he used his pseudonym, S. Q. Lapius. Its use involved no secrecy, but there was an inconsistency in its use. Various forms of his name, J. B. Naylor; J. B. Naylor, M.D.; and Dr. J. B. Naylor, identify a number of poems and stories, reflecting the author's uncertainty in establishing an identity as a writer. By 1900, he dropped the pseudonym and became consistent in the use of his full name, James Ball Naylor, in identifying his work.

JAMES BALL NAYLOR

A number of short stories are identified this way in popular magazines, including those about Jim Whiss. A series of five character sketches featuring Jim Whiss appeared in *National Magazine* from January through October, 1903. These stories are much better written than his earlier stories. Jim Whiss was an eccentric character of whom Naylor was very fond. Although Whiss was only the narrator in most of the sketches, the author's ability to describe his gestures and appearance so precisely makes him one of Naylor's more outstanding personalities.

"A Lucky Opal," among the last of Naylor's short stories, appeared in *National Magazine* in July, 1903. Young Dr. Fred Dunbar is called upon to treat a mysterious young woman under odd circumstances. Although he is not permitted to see her veiled face, he notices a birthmark on her arm and an opal ring on her finger. When he encounters the girl months later, his curiosity is aroused even more. In trying to unravel the mystery, he falls in love with her.

Naylor diverges from his usual characterization of the hero. Dunbar has few negative qualities, but neither does he have lofty attributes that detract from his personality. Actions and words make him more acceptable than was true of some of Naylor's earlier heroes, reflecting further Naylor's growth as a writer.

The use of an opal in this story was a special tribute to his wife, Villa. Before his manuscripts were submitted for publication, she copied his stories in her beautiful Spencerian handwriting, and he appreciated her assistance. When their finances eventually permitted, he gave her the equivalent of a stenographer's pay. The first thing she bought with the money was an opal tie pin for him. She took pride in his personal appearance and in her role as his helpmate by always keeping his clothing neatly pressed. The pin added a special touch, and he wore it proudly.

"The Undoing of Old John Chaney," another of the author's very touching stories, appeared in the *Ohio Magazine* in 1906. Old John, an unapproachable and hard man, is feared and disliked by most of the villagers, but when a family new to the village moves in, things change. Their two youngsters are not disturbed by his brusque manner. To the amazement of the neighbors and to old

John himself, the children work their way into his heart, causing a remarkable change in his personality. The townspeople's attitude toward Chaney and his reaction to them is much the same as the attitude of Babylon toward Dr. Barwood in *Ralph Marlowe*.

Naylor's ability to observe and interpret human values in the people around him and his skill in describing their mannerisms, their speech, and their attire continued to provide him with material used in constructing characters. Many were composites of actual people with whom he rubbed shoulders daily. He took liberties with his pen, but few people took offense with what he wrote.

He submitted a manuscript of "A Counterfeit Coin" for serialization in the *Ohio Magazine* in 1907, and it appeared in two volumes of the magazine, the first at the end of the year and the last at the beginning of 1908. The frontispiece of the first volume is a full-page portrait of the author.[136] The original manuscript bears the same title but with S. Q. Lapius as the author, indicating that it was written at least ten years prior to its actual publication. The manuscript was revised extensively before its publication.

In this narrative, Naylor again departed from his usual style by creating a main character not related to the medical profession, and one who was less of a stereotype. Doudna Run, a short distance from the Naylor home in Malta, is undoubtedly the locale of the story. While on vacation, Claude Raymond, a secret service agent, meets a charming young schoolteacher whom he suspects may be involved in counterfeiting. The agent falls in love with her, although he does not realize it until much later. Naylor handled the love story very well, and he enhanced his characterizations. The story captures and sustains the reader's interest with suspense that continues from chapter to chapter.

Naylor frequently juggled several projects at once, including *From Jim to Jack*. With a subtitle "Letters to an Old Time Schoolmate," *Jim to Jack* was published serially in the *Ohio Magazine* in 1906. The series of semi-autobiographical letters provided Naylor a means for reminiscing about his early years.[137] Proud of his humble beginnings, he sought to impart the aura of his boyhood years. While the characters were mildly disguised with fictional identities, Naylor was actually writing about himself and his long time friend, Link Kean. The series was published the following year as a booklet.

Naylor discovered early that collected verse did not sell very well, but he found ways to market individual poems. A number of his best known poems were published as broadsides. "The Muskingum Valley" and "Old Morgan County" both appeared as pamphlets designed for Christmas gifts. "Dr. John Goodfellow—Office Upstairs" appeared in several formats. Many of these were sold to friends at Naylor's office or through a local store or bank, providing a modest supplement to his income.

"Dr. John Goodfellow—Office Upstairs" was the most widely known poem written by Naylor. This poem brought a tear to many an eye, especially when he recited it with his usual flair for drama. The poem first appeared in Joe Mitchell Chapple's *National Magazine* in December, 1905, and was an immediate success. The poem was quickly picked up and carried in newspapers throughout the United States, but it was surrounded by controversy for many years. The author never claimed the story behind the poem was original, but Naylor's poem brought the story itself into national prominence.

DR. JOHN GOODFELLOW—OFFICE UPSTAIRS

> Roofed o'er by the blue of the near-bending sky,
> And walled in by the gray of grim mountain-peaks high,
> Bryson, a mountaineer's village, stands stiff
> With its front to the highway, its back to the cliff;
> A smithy it has, a postoffice, a store,
> A few humble dwellings—so much and no more.
> And lo! its inhabitants simple and shy
> Live close to the soil—and live close to the sky.
>
> Many long years ago—fully a score,
> A stairway outside of the quaint village store
> Led straight to the bare dusky room just above—
> Like a highroad of hope to a haven of love;
> And down at the foot of that stairway there swung

Theresa Marie Flaherty

A battered old sign, and this message it flung
To all who were burdened with ills or with cares:
"Dr. John Goodfellow—Office Up-Stairs."

"Dr. John Goodfellow!" Lowly was he—
Out at the elbow and out at the knee;
But though he was tousled and tattered and old,
His sinews were steel and his heart was pure gold.
Seldom a storm roistered by in its might,
But it found him abroad on the road—day or night;
Never a tortuous trail, but it led
To some sick woman's side or some little child's bed.

"Office Up-Stairs!" Ah, that small dusty den
Was the home of the saddest and gladdest of men!
His thoughts were his children, his wife was the Wild—
And his heart overflowed when in summer she smiled;
No gold had he gathered, no gear had he won—
His wealth was the mem'ry of noble deeds done;
But he bottled up gladness—and sold it in shares
Signed: "Dr. John Goodfellow—Office Upstairs."

He died--as the best and the worst of us must!--
And his friends bore him out of the dusk and the dust
Of his squalid surroundings, and laid him to rest
In the lap of the Wild he had always loved best;
Then they sold at vendue, as a matter of course,
His meager effects,—his poor bony old horse,
His black saddle-bags, his few books!—to defray
The expenses incurred when they laid him away.

Gone! Gone and forgotten! Ah, no—no! Instead
As they loved him when living, they loved him when dead;
And his grave must be marked,—though no tablet or stone
Marked a single low mound of their blood or their own!
But, untutored and crude, they were quite at a loss
How to letter his name on the rude rugged cross
At the head of his grave,—how to carve a scant line!—
Till the thought came to them of his battered old sign.

That battered old sign! Ah, they took it and nailed
It high on that cross, but they stupidly failed
To note that it served as a sign-board of love

On the road leading straight up to heaven above!
Inspired were they, but they knew it not then—
Inspired of God, those poor primitive men!
For that old sign announced:--as the Scripture declares!—
"Dr. John Goodfellow—Office Up-Stairs!"

So there in the heat of the midsummer noon—
And there in the chill of the midwinter moon,
Marking the foot of the Ladder of Light
That ends in the Land of Omnipotent Right,
Swings that old sign—as in seasons of yore
It swung at the side of Jim Miliken's store;
Still offering solace and answering pray'rs:
"Dr. John Goodfellow—Office Up-Stairs!"

The circumstances under which the author first learned the story are well known. Edmund Vance Cooke, the poet, and professional humorist "Sunshine" Hawks, were regulars on the Chautauqua circuit and visited the Naylor home on many occasions. One afternoon when they were both guests at Elmhurst, one of them recalled reading a newspaper account about an old country doctor who died a pauper. Friends and neighbors buried him, marking his grave with the sign that pointed to his second floor office.

"If you men will let me have that story, I'll make a poem out of it," Naylor said.[138] All three were enchanted with the story, and decided to flip a coin to see who would use it. Naylor won. He wrote a tender poem about Dr. Goodfellow's charity to the poor, and how he cared for the town's deadbeats and needy. Dr. Goodfellow made little money and, upon his death, his few possessions were sold to pay his debts and the simple funeral expenses. With nothing to mark his grave, those who remembered his kindness prepared a rude cross as evidence of their love and, instead of an inscription or epitaph, the sign from the doctor's office, very much like the one pointing to Naylor's second story office in Malta, was placed upon the cross without realization of the deeper significance of the words "Dr. John Goodfellow—Office Upstairs."

After the appearance of Naylor's poem, the story was modified and used by others. On one occasion, Naylor's poem was recited by someone at Chautauqua in McConnelsville and attributed it to another poet.

Theresa Marie Flaherty

Edmund Vance Cooke was in the audience and interrupted by shouting, "I beg your pardon. You gave the wrong man credit for that poem. It was written by a man who lives across the river in Malta. His name is James Ball Naylor."[139]

Miffed by recurring instances of plagiarism, Naylor wrote:

> I wrote my poem, 'Dr. John Goodfellow—Office Upstairs,' in 1905; it was published in Joe Mitchell Chapple's National Magazine, Boston; and went into my volume of verse, 'Songs from the Heart of Things,' in 1907.
>
> I have no objection to the speakers and entertainers using my stuff; but I wish they would not distort it nor seek to improve upon it—and would give credit where credit is due.[140]

Figure 7.1 - Naylor's Office Upstairs. Courtesy of Rick Shriver.

The story was also used in the 1947 movie, *The Farmer's Daughter*, starring Loretta Young, who won an Academy Award for Best Actress in this role. She was practicing her elocution and pulled a book from a shelf and read the story of Dr. Sorenson. According to Miss Young, the story was an addition to the script when they were half way through the shooting.[141]

In 1962, Hank Snow, referred to in a *National Geographic Magazine* article as "an elder statesman of Nashville's best known institution...

the Grand Old Opry," recorded "Old Doc Brown" for an RCA record, "The One and Only Hank Snow." This touching verse, told by Hank Snow against a musical background of the hymn "Just a Closer Walk With Thee," has been widely distributed on records and tape. "Old Doc Brown" was another version of Dr. John Goodfellow.

The letters Naylor wrote in *From Jim to Jack* led to another project, *Old Home Week*. Poetry, as always, was dear to his heart, and he was as anxious as ever to publish a book of his poems that would sell well. *Old Home Week* was first published in 1906 by C. M. Clark Publishers in Boston, Massachusetts, the publishers of another of his novels, *The Kentuckian*. In a poem of thirty stanzas, Naylor reveals the heartfelt sentiment of a city worker returning to his hometown after many years. The following verse was the dedication:

> To a sunburnt rogue of the Barefoot Tribe.
> Who knew every scene that I here describe.
> Every sunny glade, every shady nook!
> I dedicate this little book.
> To a brave of the Barefoot Tribe of Glee,
> To the Little Boy that I used to be!"

The pleasant home scenes, the parents' greeting of their prosperous son from the city, and the meeting of old friends recounting their boyhood experiences are thoughtfully portrayed.

The inspiration for the book was a well-known annual event founded in 1898 by Frank W. Rollins, a former governor of New Hampshire, an event that continues to this day.[142] Rollins sought to bring back the best and the brightest, those who had left for the big cities and the Midwest and beyond, decimating the rural and small town populations.

He explained, "I thought that by getting the people back every year their interest would be so increased that they would perhaps make the old town where they were born at least their summer home and spend more of their money and energy in building it up."[143]

Theresa Marie Flaherty

In his first year as governor, Rollins, under the auspices of the State Board of Agriculture, brought together "several hundred people representing all sections of the state."[144] They adopted a constitution and drew up by-laws. Their intention was to invite everyone who ever resided in New Hampshire and their descendants to return. As governor of the state, Rollins issued the following invitation:

> COME BACK AGAIN
> "But far more bright, more dear than all,
> That dream of home, that dream of home."
> OLD HOME WEEK IN NEW HAMPSHIRE.
> August 26 to September 1, 1899.
> "How dear to my heart are the scenes of my childhood."
> STATE OF NEW HAMPSHIRE - EXECUTIVE DEPARTMENT[145]

The results far exceeded Rollins expectations. Not only did the people come, but many either took up temporary or permanent residence. Many who had not visited for decades were drawn back and went on to contribute to the building of roads, schools, and libraries in their hometowns. Others planted trees, started parks, repaired churches, etc. The celebration was so successful in New Hampshire that it was adopted in Massachusetts, Maine, Vermont, and Connecticut and even in Canada. Many towns in those states and others continue to celebrate the event today.

With the Old Home Week celebrations so popular, Naylor recognized another opportunity. After the initial publication, two variations of his *Old Home Week* were published the following year, in 1907. One was printed for Frank Rollins himself, the other for John Fitzgerald, then mayor of Boston. The title pages of both are the same, bearing the date 1907. The page to the left of each title page bears a double copyright, 1906 and 1907, by C. M. Clark. The frontispiece of the New Hampshire variant carries a picture of the former governor with illustrations from scenes in New England, including his mansion, and the cover is a deep green with gold lettering.

Mayor Fitzgerald's picture appears in the Boston variant with scenes of historic importance around other cities in Massachusetts as well, including the Old North Church and the House of Seven Gables in Salem. Pasted on the inside of the front cover was a card bearing the following words, "Compliments of John F. Fitzgerald, Mayor of Boston." It was used in books given as gifts to friends and political allies by the grandfather of President Kennedy. The cover of the Boston variant is light blue with gold lettering.

As always, Naylor was deeply involved in all aspects of its production. The original illustrations, done by F. Gilbert Edge for the 1906 edition, failed to reflect the author's sentiments. Drawings by William Kirkpatrick replaced them in both variations, although the page decorations by Edge were included in all editions. The substitution is noted on the title pages of the two variants, "Illustrations by William Kirkpatrick and others," probably expressing Naylor's disapproval with the Edge illustrations.

A limited number of the original edition was printed for the author on high-grade paper with exceptionally fine binding. Those printed for public distribution were less ostentatious. Judging from the number of copies of all three of these editions that are available today, *Old Home Week* was perhaps his most successful book of poetry.

With the financial success of *Old Home Week,* Naylor optimistically began another poetry project. On May 8, 1907, Naylor signed an agreement with the Ohio Library Company of Columbus for publication of a volume of collected verse, proclaimed by the publisher, "The book is going to be the MOST BEAUTIFUL book ever issued in Ohio."[146]

The contract was the culmination of many weeks of work for Naylor. Plans called for the volume

Figure 7.2 - Naylor, the Author. Courtesy of The Morgan County Historical Society.

to be available by December 10th. The author looked forward with considerable anticipation to its appearance. By mid-November he expressed concern about the progress of the book. "It simply <u>must</u> be out in good time for the holidays; and, as I see it, you've got to rush things from this on or you'll not make it.... I've had the sale of two books partly spoiled by having them out too late for the holiday trade, and I'm nervous over the deliberation of your printers."[147] His concern was justified as the books did not arrive until Christmas day.[148] A stipulation in the contract gave him the sole right of sale in Morgan County, and he expected that delivery before Christmas would enhance sales.

"A Buckeye Rosary," Naylor's suggestion for the title, was changed to "Songs From the Heart of Things," by L. H. Bulkley, the company's representative, a substitution that pleased the author. When Bulkley suggested dividing the introductory poem; however, Naylor objected emphatically:

> Don't divide the introductory poem; it will do all right as it is—all together in the front of the volume. The 'Le Envoi' means a summing-up; and the meaning of the poem as a whole is that the Year—as to many mortals!—sings blithely and thoughtlessly, more or less, throughout the glad months of Spring and Summer, but when late Autumn comes he pensively sits down to croon and think and tell his beads. There'll be no more beautiful or truthful poem in the book, nor one that I'll feel prouder over.[149]

> *The mist of the morn—and the red orb of day;*
> *The old-home shore and your boyhood bay!*
> You up with the anchor and gallantly ride
> Afar and away on the glistening tide;
> But ever there comes like a tremulous hail,—
> On the breath of the calm, in the teeth of the gale,—
> Rising clear o'er the wide waters' silence or roar,
> The sound of a song on the old-home shore.
> *The glare of the noonday—and burning sand;*
> *And a busy mart on a foreign strand!*

You buffet the billows of dust and heat,
And you wrestle with men on the crowded street;
But there comes as you jostle your way along
In the midst of the sweltering unwashed throng,—
Like incense you knew in the days of yore,—
The faint smell of flow'rs on the old-home shore.
The dusk of the eve—and the sea below;
And the sky above, and the afterglow!

As you saunter on deck lost in thought profound,
You whistle a tune of the homeward bound;
But, again and again, you lift your eyes
Toward the darkling west where your best hope lies—
Where a few soft rays come shimmering o'er
The waves, from a light on the old-home shore.[150]

Because artwork in previous volumes disappointed Naylor, for this book he provided a large number of photographs that he had taken. The book, printed by the New Franklin Printing Company of Columbus, contained thirty-three illustrations, some watercolors, photo prints, and half tones. The more expensive editions contained a number of hand-painted photo prints. The regular edition sold for five dollars, the deluxe editions for seven and a half dollars and for ten dollars.

The Ohio Library Company worked out an extensive advertising campaign using glowing testimonials received from John Uri Lloyd of Cincinnati, Nixon Waterman and Dr. A. E. Winship of Boston, and Edmund Vance Cooke of Cleveland. Favorable comments also appeared in the *Columbus Dispa*tch, the *Cincinnati Commercial-Tribune*, and other Ohio newspapers.

John Uri Lloyd, whom Naylor had not yet met, responded to Naylor's request for a review with a charming letter that included a heartfelt invitation to Naylor. "Can I not hope to meet you some day? Are you never in this city? Would it not please you to take a trip as my guest down into my 'Stringtown' Kentucky home? Think, come."

He closed his letter with a more appropriate and usable summary:

Theresa Marie Flaherty

"Songs From the Heart of Things" is one of the most human, touching, delightful books I have ever read. It touches one deeply, I consider it a gem in word and setting. It should be on every table in every home where young and old alike live to think of love and home and life. I thank you for having written it, and I congratulate the American people on having received it.[151]

The *Ohio Magazine* reviewed *Songs From the Heart of Things* in the February 1908, issue:

Dr. Naylor is a Buckeye, almost before he is anything else. He believes in Ohio and feels the inspiration of her hills and valleys, her streams and woods. The spirit of Ohio breathes in almost all his lines, and he finds here themes for prose or poetry such as have long lain open to discovery but sadly neglected, through ignorance or lack of appreciation by other writers.[152]

This volume sold better than his first two books of poetry. However, even with all the effort that he put into its production and his own hard work as a salesman, its success did not quite live up to his high expectations. Poetry was his greatest love, and another disappointment in this arena was especially hurtful.

For many years, he designed and wrote verses for his family's Christmas cards. Inevitably, friends and neighbors asked him to design cards for them. In 1911 and 1912, four beautifully illustrated Christmas card booklets he wrote were copyrighted and published by Rust Craft of Kansas City, Missouri. These Christmas poems are among the outstanding published items emanating from his pen.

The author, always quick to recognize business opportunities, made the most of his association with Bulkley of the Ohio Library Company, publishers of *Songs From the Heart of Things*. One of his poems, "The Woodpecker," appeared in a book now quite scarce, the *Birds of Ohio*, released by the Ohio Library Company. The publishing firm at the same time used another of Naylor's poems, "The Bird's Invitation," in advertising the book.

JAMES BALL NAYLOR'S NEW BOOK
"Songs from the Heart of Things"

Is a "BEAUTY" from cover to cover. 85 Exquisite Poems -- Naylor's Life Work -- with Water-Colors Photo-prints, Halftones, all made in richest and most unique designs from ORIGINAL PHOTOGRAPHS -- THIRTY-THREE in all illustrate its sumptuous pages

JOHN URI LLOYD: One of the most human, touching, delightful books I have ever read.
NIXON WATERMAN: It goes directly to the heart of all those living, loving, normal natures that are soothed or stirred by the master poet's lines.
COLUMBUS DISPATCH: The collection is one of the best arrays that has appeared in many years.
CINCINNATI COMMERCIAL-TRIBUNE: He traverses the whole range of human experience. It is as natural for him to express his ideas in beautiful poetic rythm as for the sun to shine.

 (Send for Illustrated Sample Pages -- See Bottom of Page)

"The Birds of Ohio"

320 in number, Are all described by OHIO'S GREAT BIRD STUDENTS, from Actual Experiences with the "Birds," in their Unique and Fascinating Bird Book, Ready for distribution to readers of THE OHIO MAGAZINE

Reads like a romance. Has **80 Full Page Colored Plates** (8x10), Showing Birds in Natural Colors. **216 Original Ohio Pictures of Birds and Nests, IDENTIFICATION KEYS Migration Tables.** (Both Scientific and Popular). Cost $12,000 to produce it. $14,000 worth sold already. "The Court of Last Resort on Ohio Birds."

 (Send in the " Inquiry Coupon " Below)

THE OHIO LIBRARY COMPANY, Columbus, Ohio,
Publishers of Naylor's Poems, and "Birds of Ohio."

Please send me Full Particulars regarding these books and how to secure them. (Mention if you want to see one or both.)

Book wanted: ....

Name: ....

Address: ....

Figure 7.3 - Ad for Songs From the Heart of Things.

Local businesses occasionally purchased advertising ideas suggested by Naylor, and he solicited business from larger metropolitan areas. One of his most successful advertising poems was written for the Flinch Card Company in 1912. A very popular card game invented in 1912 by A. J. Patterson, a New York man, Flinch was first marketed in 1892.[153] Later, the owners increased the size of the pack, rewrote the rules, and promoted it using Naylor's poem. His lengthy poem in dialect is about folks in "Clovertown" who play Flinch. Published as a small pamphlet, it was included with the game. The Parker Brothers game, without Naylor's poem, is still popular today and has been updated for today's generation by the addition of wild cards.

"Angelina's Ardent Lovers" was an advertising poem similar to "Flinch" about a young woman unable to decide between two men vying for her hand in marriage. Her father decides that she will marry the first to provide a furnished home for her. One suitor begins to save his money earnestly to fulfill the father's requirement, but the other visits the "Blank, Blank Credit House," to whom Naylor had aimed his advertising effort. Although copyrighted in 1911, it apparently never sold[154]. A poem about "Lucky Strike" was sent to the American Tobacco Company, and it did sell. There were doubtless others.

In 1911 Naylor teamed up again with his friend Westerman, cartoonist for the *Ohio State Journal*, to design a special booklet for the Zanesville United Commercial Travelers Convention to be held in Zanesville. A brief history of Zanesville with pictures of places of interest in the city, each accompanied by a stanza of poetry, is included in the booklet. The frontispiece of the odd-sized booklet is "The Girl From Zanesville," an original watercolor painting by Howard Chandler Christy whom Naylor encouraged as a boy to pursue an artistic career. When Howard Chandler Christy was seventeen he came to Naylor for advice. He wanted to be an artist, but his father wanted him to remain on the farm. Remembering his own discouragements, Naylor told the boy, "Don't be discouraged. If you were born to be an artist, all the cornfields in the world will not head you off. Get good materials and go to work. You will evolve a Christy style, but you will have to do it."[155]

8
Writing for a Younger Audience

The Naylor children were often the inspiration for their father's writing. Early in 1904, Jean was just a baby, Robert was six; Lena, eight; Annie, ten; Lucile, twelve, and Olive was fourteen. Encouraged by his "pixy band," Naylor wrote an enchanting story for children that year, "Witch Crow and Barney Bylow." It appeared serially in *National Magazine* from December, 1904, through April, 1905.

Barney, a twelve-year-old boy and the son of a farmer, is dissatisfied with life at home and feels abused because of all the chores he must do. Distracted by a pesky crow, he chases the annoying bird, leaving his work behind. Exhausted from the heat and chase, he lies down to rest for a moment and falls asleep. A hoarse cawing awakens him hours later. Fearful of punishment, he runs away from home and soon encounters the crow again. The crow changes into a mysterious witch who questions him at length about his wishes. He tells her that he would like to have money in his pocket all the time, leading to unexpected complications. She gives him a penny, telling him cryptically that he will never have more, and he will never have less.

Before long, he finds himself continuously in and out of trouble because of his wish. He pulls penny after penny out of his pocket, and as long as he does not touch them again, they remain. But when he

Theresa Marie Flaherty

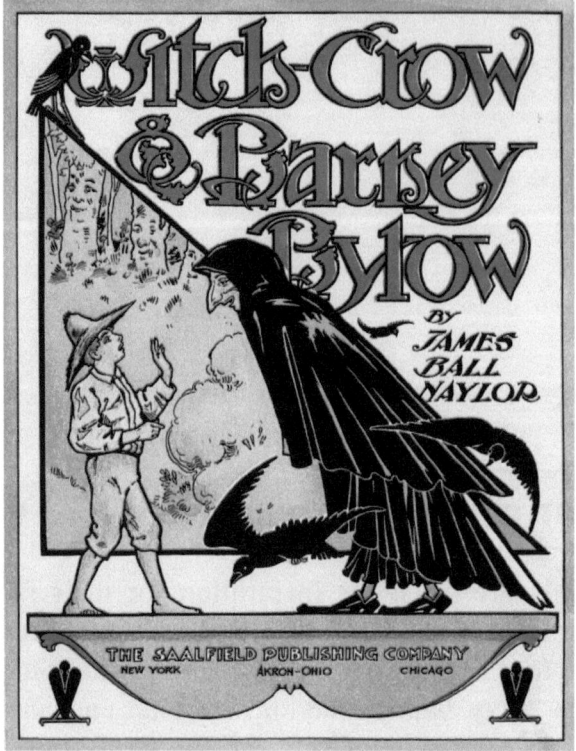

Figure 8.1 - Witch Crow & Barney Bylow.

tries to gather them together, they all disappear, making it difficult for him to pay for meals and other needs. To complicate matters, shopkeepers suspect that he is one of a gang of boys accused of stealing. When Barney meets a boy his age, he gives his newfound friend the pennies to buy something for them, but both end up in serious trouble. The consequences provide a lesson worth learning.

The following year a second story, "The Little Green Goblin of Goblinville," appeared serially in *National Magazine* in September and October, 1905. Bob Taylor, the hero in this story, also finds life miserable with too much work and too little time for play. Fitz Mee, the little green goblin, appears in Bob's room late one evening and persuades Bob to go with him to Goblinville where boys do as they please. Bob is greatly impressed with this plan. After swallowing a magic pill that shrinks him as small as his companion, he leaves with Fitz Mee in a strange balloon. Their journey is exciting, and they survive many adventures.

When they arrive in Goblinville, Bob quickly learns the customs of the strange country under unhappy circumstances. When he announces that he could use a good long sleep, he is dismayed to discover that the laws of the land require him to go to sleep immediately. Other things do not turn out to his liking either, for once he begins a task he is compelled to finish it. A wiser boy, Bob is anxious to return to the home he now appreciates.

Following serialization of the first two stories, Naylor was criticized because many words were difficult for young children to read, even though the stories themselves were captivating. Older children could read the books themselves, but those who could not appealed to their parents or brothers or sisters. Naylor's daughter Jean said, "I did hear Daddy say once that some people complained that the words were too big for children. He said he thought children ought to learn the new words rather than write down to their age level."[156]

Saalfield published both stories in hardback. *Witch Crow and Barney Bylow* appeared in 1906. *Little Green Goblin* was published the following year, but it was revised and expanded. The end of the fourth chapter was changed and five new chapters were inserted. The last three chapters remain as in the magazine, but the title was shortened. The public welcomed this additional facet of the author's talents and generously received the books.

Naylor added one more book for children to this genre. Although *Dicky Delightful in Rainbow Land*, the last of Naylor's books for children, was completed in September 1907, Saalfield did not publish it until 1909. Naylor indicated in his diary that he had problems in writing the book. "Dicky Delightful worries me; he refuses to do as I bid him. Perverse youngster!"[157] Three days later he was still "...having an 'L' of a time with that boy Dicky Delightful."[158]

Naylor's conception of the character was not as clear as those in his previous stories. Dicky, a more complacent lad than Bob or Barney, lacked the conflicting emotions that bothered the other two boys. This approach toned down the continuing interest in the outcome, but the exciting adventures of the additional characters who come to life from Dicky's nursery books hold the reader's interest.

Naylor's children's books received a great many favorable reviews, with one exception, a review that appeared in the *New York Sun* concerning *Witch Crow and Barney Bylow*. It may have disturbed the author, but those who knew him well suggest that he was probably amused.

> The modern child may be familiar with slang and the nether side of life as Mr. James Ball Naylor appears to assume.... The language he employs and the adventures he describes, though they may be realistic, are such as old fashioned people prefer to keep children in ignorance of. Mr. Naylor seems to toy around the edge of profanity in some of his expletives.[159]

Nothing vulgar or profane appears in any of Naylor's books or poetry, and even his adult novels were free of objectionable material of any kind. While his children admitted that their father had a "good vocabulary" and occasionally vented his anger with a choice bit of language, he never did so at home.

Events depicted in his children's books do not seem contrived as is sometimes evident in his other narratives, but a marked similarity may be noted in characterization and plot. In each story, the boy falls asleep, and the subsequent narrative is a dream. Each boy fits Naylor's description of himself as a youngster and is a reflection of his own childhood.

The illustrations, binding, decorations, and dust jacket design were important considerations in the publication of all of Naylor's books, and he was equally conscientious in those selected for his children's books. One editor called the illustrations for *Witch Crow and Barney Bylow* "...very poor, unnatural and inartistic."[160] Other reactions were contradictory. *Dicky Delightful in Rainbow Land* was referred to as "...crude in color, rather suggest the colored supplement of the Sunday papers."[161] The illustrations in all three were bright and colorful, and the artist in each instance sought to portray the writer's imaginative descriptions. Another felt the illustrator "...has done some excellent work."[162] *The Little Green Goblin* received the most favorable reviews of the three books. The illustrations were considered more appropriate and caught the idea of the story, aptly interpreting the incidents.

By the end of 1904, Naylor's son Robert was a wide-eyed boy

of seven who listened with adoration to all his father's stories. Looking at him, Naylor thought, "he's my own self over again... he's a terror! He's as mischievous and unreliable as his pater ever was; and that's saying a plenty, eh? Still there isn't anything cruel or vicious about the laddie; he's simply all boy—that's all."[163]

The boy's presence stirred Naylor's own childhood memories. It is not surprising then, that his next three novels, *The Cabin in the Big Woods*, *The Kentuckian*, and *The Scalawags*, all written when Robert was in grade school, are all stories about boys. Each reveals a boy's character and emotions with refreshing clarity.

The Cabin in the Big Woods, published by Saalfield in 1904, was Naylor's first serious effort at writing a novel after *Ralph Marlowe*. The story centers on the Gaylord family as Harry, a cousin of Sam and Fred Gaylord, arrives to spend the summer. When Harry claims that he has seen Andy Scott, their hired man, somewhere before, Andy denies it. Then Molly Gaylord discovers a letter that adds to the mystery. Sam, Fred, and Harry experience exciting adventures while they camp in the big woods. As they are hunting one night, they discover a secret cave that sets the stage for an exciting climax.

Naylor used a plot device from *Ralph Marlowe* in developing this story, one he had used in a short story as well. A lost letter, found and misinterpreted by his sweetheart, creates a difficult predicament for Andy, just as a similar situation did for Ralph Marlowe and for a character in another of Naylor's stories. The secret is similar, and in each narrative the characters suffer scorn and mistrust rather than reveal the truth. This recurring use of a similar plot device shows a weakness in Naylor's ability to construct original plots and affected the overall perception of his writing.

A year later, in 1905, *The Kentuckian* appeared. Many consider this the best of Naylor's novels. The book was dedicated: "To James Robert Naylor, 'the Laddie Abiding With Me,' this tale of sterling manhood is fondly dedicated, by his loving father—"[164]

Naylor added a new dimension by approaching the reader from the viewpoint of Tom Gaston, the twelve-year-old boy who narrates the story. By skillfully revealing Tom's emotions, the author added a moving element. Obviously pleased with his success in first person narration, Naylor used the style in his next two novels as well. The main characters in this novel also possess more depth and complexity than in any previous novel.

The *New York Times* commented on the author's skill in this respect:

> The true charm of the book lies in the skill with which the author preserves the simplicity of the narration, never permitting it to become any more subtle or elaborate, or to reflect any trait or characteristic not perceptible to the boy of twelve, from whose memories the story is woven. His dimly apprehended griefs and pleasures are more moving than melodrama.[165]

Vance Chatam, the Kentuckian, arrives at the Gaston's on a fine sorrel horse that he had bought in good faith, but soon finds that it had been stolen from a neighboring farmer. When he discovers that Tom's father, a coarse, unprincipled man, is involved with the gang of horse thieves, he is concerned for Tom and his sister Ruth. Their loyalty to their father is seriously affected, and they are plagued with conflicting emotions.

The episode about Chatam's first day as the schoolteacher parallels an incident in Naylor's own boyhood when a group of large boys attempted in vain to dethrone Jim Rusk when he was the new teacher. Similarly, Chatam stays on to teach at the district school, but unlike Rusk he did not believe that reason was superior to force.

> Vance encountered little opposition or difficulty at the outset of the term. His word was law; his desk was his throne. Of course, he had to deal with the open rebellion of a squad of large boys...who sought to carry out the high-handed and treasonable crime of dethronement, as had been their yearly custom. But Vance easily proved himself equal to the emergency; and the uprising was promptly quelled. He soundly walloped... the ringleader and his lieutenants, and thereby firmly established himself upon his throne and in favor of the rebels.[166]

JAMES BALL NAYLOR

A warm friendship blossoms between Tom and Chatam, much like the one that Naylor and Rusk enjoyed.

> What intimate and confidential talks Vance and I used to have as we trudged to and fro along the sun-baked, rain-gullied road.... I revealed to him my boyish dreams and aspirations, my immature aims and ambitions.... Yet in school he was my master, and I was pupil. Whether my conduct merited blame or praise, I received my due—just as did others. But I loved him! And he must have loved me, even then. For he bore with my incessant and silly prattle when we were alone, and always had a kind word of encouragement or advice for me.[167]

Chatam, as a fictional character, was original and not a reconstruction of any previous character, although he bears many of the characteristics of Naylor's mentor Rusk. Bill Kirk, however, bears a striking resemblance to Jep Tucker from Naylor's *Ralph Marlowe* novel, although more depth is shown in this character. A situation similar to one depicted in "One of Morgan's Men" is introduced in *The Kentuckian* when Ruth discovers that Vance's views of slavery are very different from her own.

By reverting to a period from the past and dwelling on the already widely written about issue of slavery, Naylor failed to capitalize on one of the underlying reasons for the success of *Ralph Marlowe;* readers were interested in contemporary America.

In the two years between the appearance of *The Kentuckian* and his next novel, two of his children's books and two of his books of collected verse were published. In addition, Naylor carried out a myriad of other activities. *The Scalawags*, published in 1907, used a number of elements from an early short story, "Stuff of Which Doctors Are Made," that appeared under Naylor's pseudonym. The short story deals with an inebriate father who removes his son from school to accompany him on a job in the hills. The boy realizes that his father is relying on him to keep him sober and, even though he does not succeed, it is a touching story.

Sim Hammer, a principal character in *The Scalawags*, is a strange looking man who, with his clever dog, visits the little country school

Tad Perkins attends. He befriends Tad, and several weeks later the boy runs away with his new friend. Unknown to Tad, Sim was a comedian and a close friend of his father, who was once the leader of a band on a showboat destroyed by an explosion on the Ohio River a few miles from Marietta. Both parents were killed, but Sim managed to rescue the infant son and find a home for him.

Tad is impressed and delighted with Sim, but their relationship is tested, and it deepens as they tramp through the Muskingum Valley. Sim, worldly and philosophical despite his appearance, has one great weakness, liquor, as Tad soon discovers. He learns his real identity as well. Sim, mortified by his young friend's disapproval, vows not to drink again. Sim and Tad make their way to a city where Tad meets some of Sim's old associates who try unsuccessfully to separate the two. Back in the theater, Sim finds a successful new career. Tom Donnelly, an old show business friend of Sim's, recognizes the change in the man and offers him the lead role in a play. Sim accepts Donnelly's offer with renewed confidence in his own ability because of Tad. Tad's fascination with every aspect of the theater was a reflection of Naylor's own. The dress rehearsal proved to be a spectacular feast that captivated the boy:

> The magic transformation—in the twinkling of an eye, as it were—of a rather passe young woman into a hoidenish schoolmiss of fifteen surprised and delighted me; I had been bothering my brain for days over how she could ever look the part—over why she had ever been selected for it. The brisk evolution of a mere slip of a girl into a prim and angular maiden lady of forty caused me to stare abstractedly; and the swift degeneration of an agile young man into a decrepit wretch of eighty filled me with awe and wonder.[168]

1907 was also the year that Olive, Naylor's eldest, went away to college. She left in March and was gone for six months. Naylor's diary reflects his keen sense of loss and depression. He wrote, "Took Olive to Zanesville, to enter business college. Seventeen years old—and leaving the nest! Ah! well, so it must be; but it hurts! My baby, my girl, my comrade! May the fates be kind to her—and send her back to her father and mother to still love and comfort them!"[169]

As the oldest, Olive held a special place in her father's heart and they were especially close. Her departure marked the beginning of changes in his family that would bring turmoil and heartfelt pain.

In 1908, inspired by Olive's circumstances, Naylor once again completed another novel, one that would be his last. *The Misadventures of Marjory* was dramatically different from any of his previous novels. Marjory Dawes, the main character, was a young woman Olive's age. Unlike most of his previous heroines who lacked depth, Marjory proved to be a delightful and controversial young woman. In narrating the story, she artfully reveals her attitudes and personality in what she says and in how she expresses herself.

Figure 8.2 - A friend, Robert, Lucile, Olive, Anne, Lena and Jean, about 1909.
Courtesy of Greg and Ellen Hill.

Twenty years of marriage and the presence of five daughters in his household no doubt contributed to Naylor's ability to correctly interpret a young woman's thoughts.

A willful girl much too pretty for her own good, Marjory's appeal brings out the protective instinct in men. When she receives a letter from her older brother, Jack, telling of his impending marriage, she rushes home to stop the marriage. Unable change her brother's mind, she resolves to leave again, but Jack will not allow it. Using her girlish wiles, Marjory appeals to an old southern gentleman who helps her to escape.

Safely aboard a train heading for Columbus, she overhears a conversation about a girl named Sarah Grimes, who was hired by a firm in the city. But the girl took another job without a word to the Columbus firm. Marjory decides to pass herself off as Sarah and get the position herself. Along the way she loses her purse. In desperation, she seeks a young man's help, and he pays for her ticket.

Marjory obtains the position, only to discover that her new boss is the same man who paid for her ticket. Ned Durbin hired the real Sarah Grimes, a most unattractive young lady, to discourage his father, whose inability to resist a pretty face was causing problems in the office. Despite Marjory's obvious good looks, Ned allows her to continue the deception. The father is delighted with his son's choice and, when Ned does not reveal Marjory's identity, he becomes embroiled in a complicated situation.

The elder Durbin, however, is disturbed by his son's lack of interest in the fair sex. His amorous conduct was a way of trying to ignite a spark of interest in Ned. This time he succeeds, and Marjory enjoys the game. Together she and Ned's father conspire to win over Ned.

The plot for *The Misadventures of Marjory* expands on a similar situation in an early short story, "The Blackmer Affair," but in this instance Marjory is a heroine, while Lucretia Blackmer was a despicable character. Again, Naylor borrowed an idea from another story to create this one. If he was criticized for this, he might have replied in answer, as he did upon one occasion, "For may I not do what I like with mine own production?"[170]

No details are available about Naylor's dealings with his publishers. There is no doubt that he was as involved in the decision-making process regarding his novels as he was with his books of poetry. How much he may have earned or how involved the publishers were in editing and producing his novels remains a question.[171]

Saalfield published the first five of his novels, but Naylor did not use them for the last three that were published between 1905 and 1908. Saalfield may have been displeased when he looked elsewhere for a publisher of his novels, and he may have shopped without success for another publisher for his last children's story as well. Primarily a publisher of children's books, Saalfield eventually published all three of his children's stories between 1906 and 1909, during the time frame that two other publishers published Naylor's last three novels.

Naylor may have felt that he could make a more lucrative arrangement elsewhere. In 1905, he moved from Saalfield to C. M. Clark Publishing Company, located in Boston, for *The Kentuckian*. They also published all three editions of *Old Home Week* in 1906 and 1907. Another publisher may have been suggested to Naylor by friends that he met at a writers' convention in Boston in 1906. Whatever the reason, Naylor did not use C. M. Clark for his next novel. Instead he chose the New York firm, B. W. Dodge and Company, to publish *The Scalawags* in 1907. The following year, in 1908, he returned to C. M. Clark with *The Misadventures of Marjory*.

Fate was not kind to him either when it came to his publishers. A warehouse fire at Saalfield destroyed the plates to his early books, putting a damper on much of his royalty income. He lost additional royalties from his last three novels, *The Kentuckian*, *The Scalawags*, and *The Misadventures of Marjory*, when both the C. M. Clark and B. W. Dodge companies went bankrupt.

Theresa Marie Flaherty

9

Speaker and Entertainer

Long before the era of movies and television, the public was hungry for culture and education, and speakers were in great demand on any number of literary association and Lyceum[172] circuits. Churches were the first to feed that hunger, often providing more than just religious education. The lecture circuit, comprised at first of preachers and men of the cloth who had honed their speaking skills in the pulpit, reached even the smallest villages. Other talented orators, many of them politicians, discovered that they could make a living at public speaking. Entrepreneurs launched businesses to support them, including talent bureaus and booking agencies. The enterprise was called "Lyceum," a word coined by the Greeks and taken from the "Temple of Apollo Lyceus" where Aristotle taught. Even in ancient Greece, the people gathered in the streets to listen to their unpaid philosophers and poets. When one of them at last became so popular that the people would pay to hear him, Lyceum was born.

The American Lyceum Association was created in 1831, uniting a string of lecture and debating societies. Among the notable speakers to emerge were Mark Twain, Amos Bronson Alcott, the father of Louisa May Alcott, Henry Ward Beecher, and many others. The programs on the Lyceum platform in the solemn halls of churches and libraries sought to uplift. While they may have offered bits of humor, the audiences wanted to laugh, and laugh out loud. Humorists were consigned to the less cultured opera houses and town halls, at least until about 1904 when comedy and culture were combined on the same platform in a travelling tent. A new form of "Chautauqua" was born, and a new epoch in entertainment emerged.

Figure 9.1 - Muskingum Valley Chautauqua. Courtesy *The Morgan County Herald*.

Chautauqua became more than just the name of a county, a lake, and an institution in southwestern New York state. The institution began in 1874 as a Sunday school assembly and religious summer camp with an array of activities that grew to include education, art, music, theater, sports, and much more. Independent Chautauquas sprang up in towns across the country, where they held camp-style meetings every summer for many years. McConnelsville, across the river from Naylor's Malta, held a ten-day Chautauqua in July/August every summer for twenty-six years, from 1906 to 1932.[173]

There was a definite difference between Lyceum and Chautauqua. Lyceum was the somber cousin of Chautauqua. Lyceum lectures were held in churches, schools or libraries, and delivered from a platform. Topics might be amusing, but they elicited chuckles rather than belly laughs. Chautauqua was show business through and through, using a stage set up in tents that were pitched in pastures and on the town square. Oratory was offered, but so were music, drama, art lessons, and cooking classes.[174]

Theresa Marie Flaherty

Chautauquas were big events and a big stimulus to the local economies. Each locale had its own way of managing them. Keith Vawter, the western manager for the Redpath Lyceum Bureau, developed a weeklong traveling tent circuit that reduced overhead and improved conditions for the performers. With nine tents for a seven-day program in

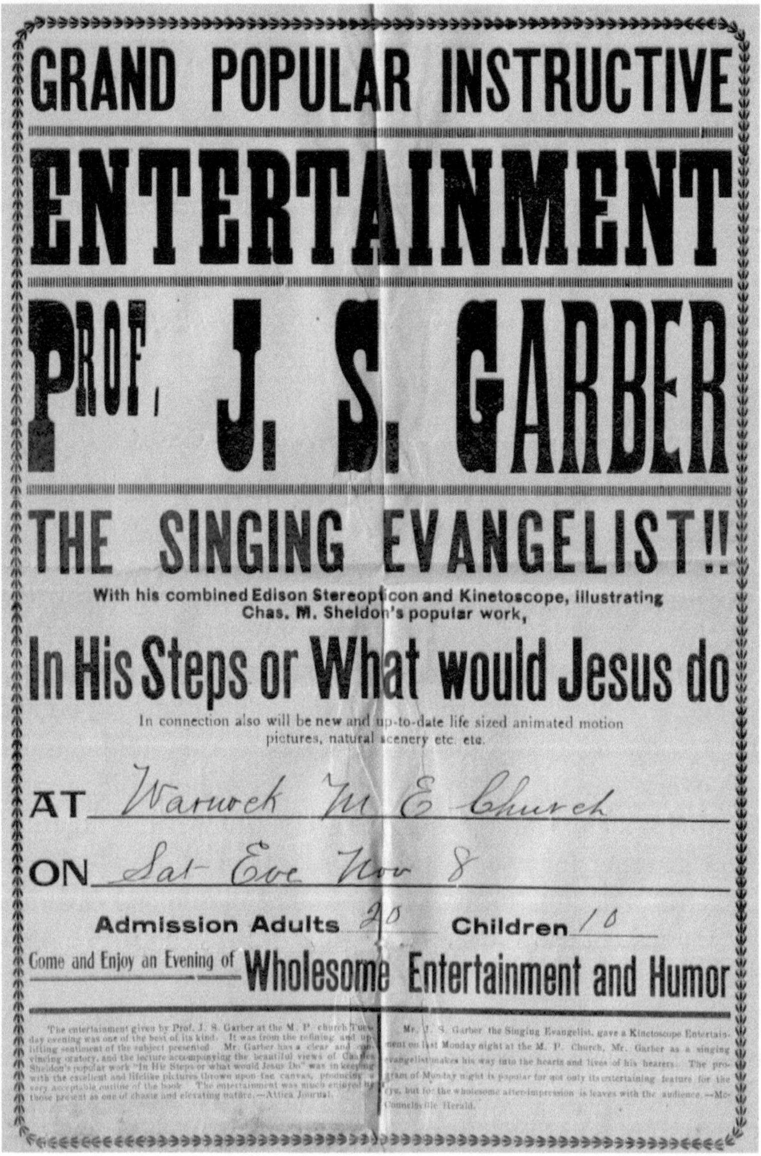

Figure 9.2 - J.S. 1890 Poster for Prof. J.S. Garber. Courtesy of D.W. Garber.

eight locations, each crew set up one of the tents in another town along the circuit, leapfrogging over eight towns to arrive in the new location with a full day to spare. No matter what day a program started, the talent that performed on the first day in one performed the first day in each town along the circuit.[175]

For the next twenty-five years, Chautauqua and Lyceum existed side by side, often using the same talent, and often operated by the same men. Their demise came in the early 1930s with the advent of the automobile, radio, and movies.

Although Naylor appeared at Chautauquas occasionally, he was not a regular on the circuit. His talent was more suited to individual appearances on the Lyceum circuit where he was the sole performer. His diaries reveal that he often performed several times a month or more. A great many people throughout the state and beyond knew Naylor from his "platform" work as a speaker and entertainer. This area of his work was much more extensive than previously known.[176] From the appearance of his earliest poems, his poetry was received enthusiastically, and he was asked frequently to recite his poems. No one could duplicate his ability in this respect for he delivered each line with exactly the right rhythm and emphasis. He was already known as a gifted speaker in political circles. As he developed his programs, his ability as a speaker increased, extending far beyond merely reading his own productions.

As a youngster he loved the circus, where he encountered professional entertainers for the first time. He attended every one when possible and learned a great deal from them. He firmly believed that "the kiddos will get more real education—more of the inspiration that stimulates the growth of gray matter in the summit of the calvarium—than they could possibly get in the school-room in the same length of time."[177]

The traveling circuses that visited the country towns then were one-ring shows, and always, there was a clown to captivate the audience. Dan Rice, an outstanding performer whom Naylor admired as a boy, was the ringmaster, strongman, equestrian, and clown. He also sang, danced, and performed what would today be called stand-up comedy. At the height of his popularity in the 1860's, Dan Rice was as well known as P. T. Barnum. Initially, the circus was geared to adults, and Rice was skilled in bantering with his audiences. He became well known beyond the circus from his political commentaries, and at one point he campaigned from the circus ring for Pennsylvania State Senate as a Peace Democrat and even ventured briefly into the 1868 presidential campaign.[178]

In Naylor's poem "The Dan Rice Show," he reveals his joy in contemplating a visit to the circus, and it clearly depicts the locale where he grew up and spent his entire life. Written more than thirty years after visiting Dan Rice's circus, this stanza from the poem illustrates the poet's faculty for recalling details of bygone days.

> Daylight jest a-comin'—an' the road a-stretchin' gray
> 'Cross the hills to Rokeby half a dozen miles away—
> Seen me on my travels' feelin' mighty big an' grand,
> A dollar in my pocket an' a doughnut in my hand.
> W'en I'd got to Douda Run an' town was drawin' near,
> Circus horns a-tootin' fell upon my waitin' ear;
> Roads was jammed an' crowded—people surgin' to an' fro,
> All a-trav'lin down to Rokeby to the Dan Rice Show.
> *It was right foot, left foot—*
> *Trigged up spruce an' nice;*
> *Lookin' fer the circus,*
>   *An' fer Ol' Dan Rice!*[179]

By the time that *Current Coins*, Naylor's first volume of poetry, appeared in 1893, his poetry had appeared in newspapers and magazines throughout Ohio, and he had given dozens of readings throughout Morgan County and elsewhere. By then he had prepared a broadside to advertise "An Evening with S. Q. Lapius," using the same photograph as the one included in the book. By supplementing his readings with an introductory talk on dialect poetry and providing explanatory remarks regarding each poem, Naylor quickly developed a rapport with his audiences.

His entertainments were often booked as part of a lecture series and, although referred to as such, he preferred that they be called simply "talks."[180] In appearing before various groups, Naylor often used exaggerated facial expressions to accentuate his readings. His voice was strong and clear, his gestures expressive, and his enthusiasm put a zest into his evening's work that won him many favorable reviews. His ability to pass so easily from the sublime to the ridiculous delighted his audiences. Many testimonials appeared in contemporary newspapers during his active years as an entertainer confirming the public's acceptance of his efforts.

One such testimonial emphasized the charming manner with which S.Q. Lapius presented his productions:

> ...who not only writes the most humorous and the most pathetic of poems, but recites them in such a manner as to put his audience quite in touch with himself and moves it to see that about which he is talking, and feel the pathos or the humor somewhat as he must have felt it when he put his thoughts into rhyme."[181]

Lucile described her father as "...never so happy and at ease as when on his feet facing an audience." She said that he faced his most difficult audience early in his career in Chesterhill, a Quaker town not far from his home. He worked very hard to get the reserved Quaker audience to laugh at his antics, but without success. After the entertainment was over and he was enjoying the congratulations, a friend said to him, "James, if thee hadn't quit thy foolishness right when thee did, thee'd have had us all laughing."[182]

At some point he expanded his programs to include much more than the mere reading of his own poetry. He added material that transitioned seamlessly from one poem to another yet kept within the theme of the program.

Figure 9.3 - Naylor, the Entertainer.

Theresa Marie Flaherty

"When You and I Were Boys," one of his favorite presentations, was used many times and could be adapted for the audience. He usually began the program by reciting the title poem of the entertainment and "The Song in My Heart." He followed with a touching monologue interspersed with more poetry. Leading his audience on a journey through life, he started with the boy who eagerly looks ahead to the day he is a man and able to stretch full length in a barber chair, argue politics on the street corner, cast a first ballot at the polls, and keep steady company with his best girl. Once the boy has reached manhood, he is caught up with consuming ambition, and with tireless energy he pursues success.

> He enters the marvelous City of Success; and therein takes up temporary residence. He feasts upon its garish splendors; he feeds fat upon its incalculable riches. The clang of its many bells, the shriek of its myriad whistles, the din and roar of its numerous shops and factories, is as music to his sordid soul; and its hustle and bustle, and hurry and worry, is as the breath of life to his nostrils. He takes a stand in the marketplace and elbows his competitors aside; he secures a footing upon the floor of the stock exchange—and ruthlessly tramples his opponents in the dust; with other schemers, he schemes over fabulous franchises—and greedily grasps everything that comes within his reach. And his heart is satisfied—for a day, a month, a year![183]

Too late, the man realizes that success is not what he thought it would be; he looks longingly back upon the road he traveled, regretting each milepost that he passed unseeing in his haste to reach the "City of Success." His children then set out on their own journey of life, and once again he draws closer to his own dear wife. Her beauty is now faded and her hair has turned white, but he sees her in the deceptive light of the past and finds her young and fair. Together they travel the last miles of the journey.

Given Naylor's superb sense of drama, it is easy to see how he brought tears to many in his audience. Quickly changing his routine, he told his listeners about revisiting the scenes of his boyhood and set the

Dr. James Ball Naylor

Poet, Novelist, Entertainer

UNDER AUSPICES OF

BUTLER PUBLIC SCHOOLS

AT OPERA HALL

Next Friday Evening

Dr. Naylor is the Whitcomb Riley of Ohio--A Poet and Novelist of National Reputation

He Will Read and Act His Own Poems

ADMISSION:

RESERVED SEATS 25c   **GENERAL ADMISSION 15c**

SCHOOL CHILDREN 10 CENTS

Come Everybody and Enjoy a Rare Treat

Figure 9.4 - Butler Entertainment Program. Courtesy of D.W. Garber.

stage for some of his own favorite poems, "Down at Hughes Ol' Shop," "Newton Ridge," "The Old Country Dance," and others.

Part of the script for "When You and I Were Boys" was used in *From Jim to Jack*. One section from another program, "One Country, One People, One Flag," was a stirring patriotic talk that Naylor used often to express many of his personal philosophies. It also appears in the pamphlet. Other portions of *From Jim to Jack* would have been delightful in similar entertainment programs and may well have been included in some.

Theresa Marie Flaherty

Only under dire circumstances did Naylor ever cancel an engagement once he had agreed to appear, often traveling long distances in bad weather through storms to visit remote areas in Morgan and surrounding counties. On these occasions the audiences were often sparse. While there might be only a handful of brave farmers who struggled through the storm to listen to him, he put his whole heart into his performance, and they showed their appreciation for his entertainment. On one occasion during a severe summer storm, Naylor traveled to Caldwell over the hills east of his home to fulfill an engagement. An article in the local paper commented on his performance:

> The attendance was good—considering the frightful condition of the weather. Dr. Naylor is an entertaining, as well as forceful, speaker and for nearly two hours he kept his audiences in almost continuous uproar.... Caldwell has been visited by many noted orators and lecturers but none ever gave better satisfaction or received more cordial reception than did Dr. James Ball Naylor.[184]

Early in his career Naylor was invited to entertain at a meeting of the Muskingum County Medical Society in Zanesville. His ready wit and flow of good stories captivated his professional associates. Later, when he was invited back to Zanesville to appear before the Muskingum County Teachers' Institute, the *Zanesville Times-Recorder* commented:

> ...the gifted Morgan County author and humorist, gave an entertainment which rivaled the best ever given in this city for merit, humor and the ready sympathy with the entertainer, evinced by the audience, which was at different times moved to laughter and sadness by the ready flow of phrases from the author.[185]

At an entertainment before a large audience at a Congregational church, Naylor read a number of poems from *Songs From the Heart of Things*. A newspaper article following his appearance said that "he was recalled and recalled and closed the evening's entertainment midst a very storm of applause."[186]

When appearing in a small town, Naylor adopted an old showman's technique of printing flyers at the local press to advertise his appearance in the village. Schoolboys eagerly sought the privilege of distributing the flyers to the village residents to gain free admission. Occasionally a friend or favored individual received a complimentary ticket that the author had printed for that purpose. It was something that no doubt afforded him considerable pleasure. It read:

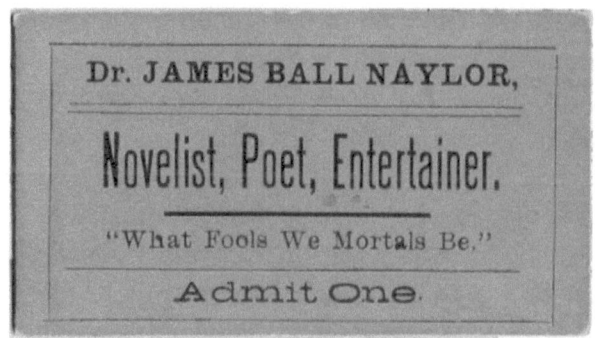

Figure 9.5 - Naylor Admittance Ticket. Courtesy of Greg and Ellen Hill.

Naylor usually received from twenty to thirty dollars and occasionally more for an appearance, and seldom lowered the fee as a special favor. When *Songs From the Heart of Things* was being published, L. H. Bulkley of the Ohio Library Company asked him to come to Columbus and give two entertainments. In this instance Naylor agreed to appear for twenty dollars and expenses, but told Bulkley to "keep that price as obscure as possible; you will readily understand that I'm making the price thus, as a favor to you...."[187] Naylor provided Bulkley with some of the circulars he had used in his platform work, with permission to prepare a new circular for the occasion.

As Naylor's reputation grew, so did the demand for his appearance. Requests came not only from Columbus, Cleveland, and other cities in Ohio, but from Chicago, Boston, and New York as well. Most of Naylor's trips to Chicago were politically motivated, but he took advantage of the opportunity to entertain there.

He attended a writer's convention in New England where he met many of his contemporaries and developed life-long friendships. The C. M. Clark Publishing Company, publishers of *Old Home Week* and others of his novels, was located in Boston, and Naylor visited them on several occasions, making appearances there as an entertainer as well.

In 1907, his good friend Harry Westerman invited him as the guest of honor at a banquet of the Harrow Club in Columbus. This unique organization was comprised of only ten members and had no rules or regulations. The meetings were regarded as "most interesting and semi-Bohemian events," and invitations were highly prized.[188] On the evening of December 22, 1907, Naylor was one of nine guests invited. E.O. Randall, the permanent chairman of the club, introduced Westerman, who became the master of ceremonies. Naylor was the principal entertainer of the evening, but several others spoke honoring him. Samuel Flickinger, one of the guests, was the first editor to receive Naylor's poems, and he recounted humorously their narrow escape from his waste basket. Charles Kinney read a poem he wrote dedicated to Naylor, Harold Simpson described events when the Republican Glee Club sang Naylor's well known verses, and Colonel Wilson of the State Journal, where much of Naylor's work was printed, added his testimony.

Another well known member of the Harrow Club was Opha Moore, an Ohio historian, to whom Naylor penned the following poem, obviously his reply when he could not attend an upcoming meeting:

>My dear Opha Moore:
>>I am taking
>In the strenuous effort of making
>>You fellows up there understand:
>That the railroads now issue no passes,
>>That they've called in the ones that I've had,
>That the highways are glue and molasses—
>>And the walking's infernally bad.
>
>However, I'm herewith remitting
>>A check for five dollars, to rub
>Out my part of the cost of your sitting—
>>And to pay for my share of the grub;
>So reserve me a peg in the hallway—
>>A mere hook for my battered old hat,

JAMES BALL NAYLOR

Just to show to your friend, in a small way,
    That you miss him—wherever he's <u>at</u>.

And when duly assembled at table,
    Kindly designate one empty chair
And indulge in the fanciful fable
    That your rhyme-jingling brother is there;
Place a plate for the poor luckless sinner,
    Who begs your indulgence to say
That he always enjoys a good dinner—
    But not in this long-distance way.

And, also, when eating and drinking,
    And laughing and chatting in glee,
Waste a wee fleeting moment in thinking
    Of him who is absent—that's me:
And should some fellow chance to unravel
    A yarn of rare worth, bear in mind
That this dull Harrow tooth scratching gravel
    Has a fondness for that very kind.

In Conclusion, when dinner is over
    And the old Harrow's ripping around—
Making paths through the blossomy clover
    And leaving its marks on the ground,
Should some fellow get hurt in the frolic,—
    Wherever that region may be!-
And give him red-pepper sauce, for the colic—
    And charge him two dollars for me.

And I'm wishing—though some in doubt whether
    I can make it quite plain in my rhyme—
That you'll have, when you all get together,
    Just a hell of a Harrowing time!
And if stern Duty wasn't my jailer—
    But there—there! I know it can't be!

So I sign myself—

Yours,

James Ball Naylor.

P.S. Save a stogie for me![189]

The Ohio Society of New York, a prestigious group of well-known men from Ohio, invited him to appear before one of their meetings in November, 1917.[190] The group met at the Waldorf-Astoria and booked him a room in the grand hotel on the fifteenth floor near their meeting room. He recited "The Good Old Buckeye State," a poem written especially for the event.[191] An editorial after his address in New York said, "There could not have been a truer guest from Ohio than Mr. Naylor and in greeting him the society welcomed one of the best poets of the state. Naylor has a rich soul that glows in a crowd of intelligent people."[192]

Unsolicited testimonials found their way into local papers throughout Ohio and as far away as New York and Boston, further attesting to his popularity. Some were quaint and sometimes emotional and highly laudatory, but all revealed the public's interest in Naylor both as an entertainer and as a man whom everyone considered a friend and neighbor.

Family Entertainers

As his children got a little older, Naylor was pleased to have them participate with him in his entertainments. Olive and Lucile were the first to take part, and before long they were seasoned performers. In an entertainment given in Caldwell in 1904 when Olive was fourteen and Lucile was twelve, they were well received:

> Dr. James Ball Naylor and daughters were here Thursday evening as advertised and not only fulfilled but exceeded any claim that was made for them. No lecture or entertainment that has been given at Caldwell has had more flattering comment. Delightful is the word. Of course a great deal was expected of Naylor and there was no disappointment.

He cracks the crust off the heart and too, with a maul of his own fashioning. But his daughters! What we might say of them would make Naylor jealous were it not all in the family. Still but children are Misses Olive and Lucile but talented and no mistake. And then such childish unaffectedness makes them charming too. They were applauded from start to finish. Caldwell will give them a house any time.[193]

Naylor signed a contract with the Lyceum Bureau of Columbus, Ohio, for the 1905-1906 season, providing an explanation for his busy schedule of appearances. Olive was sixteen and Lucile was thirteen, and they were included by name in the contract.[194] The bureau guaranteed at least ten bookings for the season, with two weeks' advance notice. They were paid from twenty to thirty-five dollars for each booking, depending on how many appearances they made in a given week. Expenses were covered, except for hotels, as Naylor agreed to accept two cents per mile per diem instead. The contract also stipulated that the bureau had first choice of his platform services for the next season.[195]

In response to those who inquired about his availability for an appearance, he mailed a very fine eight-page brochure. It included endorsements from prominent individuals, school superintendents, presidents of well-known organizations, and editors of newspapers who had enjoyed his entertainment. The brochure also contained photographs of him and members of his family.

Naylor's association with the Lyceum Bureau was obviously a successful one as it continued for a number of years.[196] Naylor's diaries identify numerous entertainments

Figure 9.6 - Naylor with Lucile and Olive.

presented throughout the next ten years. In the last six months of 1907, under the terms of this contract, he earned at least three hundred and forty-five dollars plus expenses for thirteen appearances, supplementing his income quite nicely.[197] Most of these were within thirty miles of his home, but one in Coshocton to address a meeting of the Independent Order of Odd Fellows (IOOF), a benevolent organization whose aim is to make the world a better place in which to live, was more than sixty miles away.

Professor A. E, Winship, editor of the *American Journal of Education* in Boston, and another notable speaker on the lecture circuit, said in a 1904 review that he had enjoyed "practically every important combination of entertainers staged for the lecture-going public" and had twice heard Naylor and his daughters. He said, "...without any reservation or equivocation whatever I place their evening's musical and recitative entertainment—in variety, in originality, in genius, and in personality—above anything in the market unless it be some international star."[198]

"THE NAYLORS."

At Union Hall, Malta, O.,
Friday Evening, April 17, 1908.
8 o'clock,

BENEFIT W. R. C.

Readers: Dr. James Ball Naylor, Master Robert.
Mezzo-Soprano.........Miss Olive.
Piano: Miss Olive, Miss Lucile.
Violin: Miss Olive, Miss Lucile.
Flute....................Miss Annie.
Cornet.................Miss Lena.

PROGRAM:

I. Selection--"Martha," ....*Flotow*.
Orchestra.
II. Original Readings: 'The Cumberland Stage' 'Song of the Motor Car,'
Dr. Naylor.
III. Cornet Solo--"A Dream of Paradise," .....*Gray*.
Miss Lena.
IV. Reading--"Foolin' Ma" ....*James Ball Naylor*.
Master Robert.
V. Flute Solo--"Valse Des Roses," ....*Kohler*.
Miss Annie.
VI. Vocal Solo--"Honey Town," ....*Widener and Heuman*.
Miss Olive.
VII. Original Readings ....*Selected*.
Dr. Naylor.
VIII. Violin Solo--"Serenade Badine,"-- ....*Gabriel-Marie*.
Miss Lucile.
IX. Selection--"Faust," ....*Gounod*.
Orchestra.

Figure 9.7 - 1908 Entertainment Program.

On one occasion they performed at Clark's Opera House in Toronto, Ohio, under trying circumstances. It was the first time the opera house was used that season. The fires had not been started in time, and the house was cold and damp. The audience shivered in their seats but remained to enjoy the entertainment despite their discomfort, and the Naylors gave a performance to the fair-sized crowd that "gave splendid satisfaction."[199]

Anne and Lena also joined the family troupe, as did Robert. Jean was the only one who did not because, by the time she was of an age to join them, the older children had found other interests, and her father's thoughts had turned more and more to politics and the war effort.

The girls, all talented in music and elocution, recited poetry and read both humorous and serious skits written by their father. They sang and played instruments. Olive and Lucile both played the violin and piano; Anne played the flute, and Lena the cornet. Robert, too young to join them in the earliest days, participated less than the four girls. When he finally joined the group, he recited "Foolin' Ma," a popular part of the program written especially for him. Although Robert did not play an instrument in the programs, he did study music. His father expressed his disappointment in his diary in 1907 when "Bob failed in music." Robert improved, however, and eventually played a trombone in the Army.[200]

The girls provided a musical background for their father's readings and each played solos. Naylor wrote many original poems for his entertainments, and he also adapted many that had already appeared in various publications. "The Diversions of Dicky Dare," a short story, was adapted for an entertainment program that highlighted Lucile's talents. Both Naylor and his daughters accepted and used material written by contemporaries who were his good friends. His daughters recited "Aunt Shaw's Pet Jug" by Holman Day, "In Fishing Time" by Well S. McCann, and "A Modern Washington" by Joseph C. Lincoln, as well as others by Eugene Field and James Whitcomb Riley. However, when another's material was used, Naylor always gave the author credit.

Naylor's programs appeared with titles that varied from time to time, but the content was usually much the same. Naylor's wit was sharp, and he often adapted his material to suit the situation and the audience. One of his early readings, "Heartfelt Poems and Homespun Yarns," consisting mostly of his early dialect poetry, was always received with enthusiasm. He interspersed his lectures with facetious and amusing poems that elicited much laughter, and often with a serious one that brought forth a few handkerchiefs among the more tenderhearted members of his audience.

His programs always concluded on a happy note, and afterward members of a grateful audience inundated Naylor with words of appreciation.

One enthusiastic audience at a reading at the Zanesville Masonic Temple was very appreciative.

> The genial novelist won all hearts at the very outset by his optimism, which was contagious, 'The Jester' and 'My Skies are Seldom Gray' deserve special mention. In these the good doctor embodies his optimistic views so cleverly that they become at once the creed of the audience.[201]

On one occasion, Naylor appeared at Chautauqua in Woodsfield, Ohio, where he had difficulty speaking because of a painfully sore throat. A review in the local paper said that he "is thought by some to have been the best number of the entire course."

The review continued:

> The Doctor devoted the afternoon to reading some of his poems. Every one was full of both truth and poetry. He speaks from the heart and teaches many a good lesson. He is one of the greatest entertainers on the lecture platform and when he concludes he leaves his auditors with a yearning for more.[202]

Naylor was appreciative of others' works and made his feelings known whenever possible. When he read an article about Mark Twain in the *Herald*, he dropped by the *Herald* office to convey his approval. In commenting about Naylor's visit in another article two weeks later, the editor wrote that like Twain:

> Dr. Naylor is an equally strong, robust individual. He, himself, developed a native penchant for literature; a soul sensitive to beauty found in expression in the winged words of poetry; and a gift of tongues brightened and softened with a rare dower of humor were turned to advantage on the platform. He was one of the best public speakers we ever heard, and as a raconteur must have equaled Abe Lincoln at his best. Did you

ever hear Dr. Naylor speak 15 years ago when his heart was in the war or as it was in 1916 when he believed with all his soul that the pacifism and wobbling of Woodrow Wilson was inevitably drawing us into the vortex of the world catastrophe? We heard him speak at Hackney in the Hughes-Wilson campaign in what to us will be an ever memorable occasion.[203]

Figure 9.8 - Entertainment Poster of Photos. Courtesy Greg and Ellen Hill.

Theresa Marie Flaherty

An audience's enthusiastic response and the congratulations that followed behind the scenes were experiences that Naylor enjoyed immensely. Applause provided a welcome boost to his ego, for it was a clear indication of the public's acceptance and appreciation for his talents. His keen sense of humor and innate sense of what was of human interest served him well. Had he chosen to focus his efforts in his lyceum work as a lecturer and entertainer to the exclusion of his other abilities, he might have gained worldwide fame. "No better story teller ever appeared on a public platform," said one who knew him well. "No man ever lived with a readier tongue and a quicker wit and one which could be applied to any situation which arose."[204]

Naylor's platform work with his children brought him great joy, but it brought a measure of sorrow as well. His platform work was but one facet of his genius, but for his daughter, Olive, the stage was everything. Smitten with the theater at an early age, Olive pursued a career on stage, despite her college training and to the distress of her friends and family. Naylor was the one who introduced her to the limelight, and he could not keep her from what she considered her calling. She loved the stage and left home to join a professional theatrical troupe, a move that many people in the area found disquieting. She remained with the group for six years, traveling throughout the area, "playing every part from slavey to society debutante in road shows that made all night jumps and one night stands."[205] An excellent actress, she might have made a name for herself, but instead she fell in love and married her leading man, Charles. H. Doty. When Winston and Weston, twin boys, were born in 1913, Olive left the stage. Her marriage failed dismally. Family disagreements brought heartache to them all. Left alone with twin sons, Olive sought sanctuary with her family in Malta with her boys. Just after the twins turned three, Naylor noted sarcastically in his diary, "Olive got notice from her reverant husband that he means to do nothing for her."[206]

In a possible effort to console Olive, Naylor tried his hand at writing the script for a play, "The Little Town of Toddville," about Quakers. The story revolves around the Woolman's. The father, clinging tenaciously to the beliefs and customs of the old religion, is determined that his daughter shall marry Amos Hardsole, a Quaker, rather than the man she loves who is not. Assuming an attitude of moral rectitude and smug hypocrisy, Hardsole completely deceives the old man and gains his support. While his rival is away from the village, Hardsole plans to destroy his reputation and nearly succeeds. Dr. Goodheart works toward untangling the whole affair.

Olive formed the Zweistadt Players, a group composed of local talent. In October, 1915 she directed a production of "The Little Town of Toddville," with her brother Bob, then sixteen, appearing as Jud Piper in some funny scenes. Even little Jean, at eleven, with "quaint, ingenuous ways" appeared in the production. The play was well received in the opera house at McConnelsville.[207] A week later, the play was performed in Stockport before a "good house" with an appreciative audience. The players, the Armory orchestra, and everyone involved had a great time.[208]

The twin grandsons were a delight to their grandparents. At one point, when Olive found a job in Chicago, she left the little boys with her parents, who doted on them. Much of the first five years of the boys' lives was spent at Elmhurst.

When Olive moved with the boys to Southern California to pursue a career in the movie industry, Naylor and his wife were stoic and determined to be supportive, despite their dissapointment. Olive became a stage mother and helped the twins win parts in a number of silent movies. They both appeared in the original 1922 *Our Gang* series of films, including *One Terrible Day* and *Fire Fighters*. Winston appeared in the films *Lodge Night* and *A Pleasant Journey* in 1923. Their acting careers culminated with parts in the 1924 version of *Peter Pan*.

The Naylors made a number of trips to the West Coast to visit Olive and the boys, and the boys returned to spend an occasional summer with their grandparents at Elmhurst. The twins were a blessing to their grandparents and, despite the distance, maintained a close relationship with them.

10

In the Political Arena

Running for Office

At the tender age of eight, Naylor was introduced to the world of politics during the presidential campaign of 1868. In that first presidential election after the Civil War, Republican General Ulysses S. Grant, a war hero who was considered the man who won the war, easily defeated former Governor of New York Horatio Seymour. Young Naylor was thrilled to be associated with the winning side in such an electrifying campaign. His life-long involvement in politics was sealed, so much so that he ran for public office a number of times during the years he was most prolific as a writer and poet.

Naylor, however, was exposed to political ideology long before that fateful campaign. Losing his father in the Civil War and gaining a stepfather who survived that war deeply affected the impressionable lad. In describing those Civil War soldiers who returned, he wrote:

> These Civil war soldiers simply settled down to be the best citizens the republic has ever known. They began to make things hum, industrially and commercially; they began to help in paying off the war debt; they began to take a prominent part—in fact, the leading part—in political affairs. Evidently, they felt that they had saved the country—so they were going to run the country; and they did.[209]

Of the campaigns of the 1870's and 1880's, he recalled, "Few qualified voters could be kept away from the polls, and those who showed little inclination to exercise their right to vote were 'promptly and efficiently looked after.'"[210] Politicians rounded them up, gave them marked tickets, and marched them to the ballot box. Sometimes, however, it required from two to five dollars to convince them to vote, but the money was always available and proved effective.

> Why, they used to spend more money in Morgan County—than is now spent in the whole congressional district! And it brought results; it got the vote out. Voters were not ashamed to be partisans then; no, indeed. They were either Republicans or Democrats—and nothing else; and were proud of the fact. There were no mongrels; there were no 'blocs.' A man might scratch his head over political problems; but he seldom scratched his ticket.[211]

Naylor was normally a party man, but at one election after reaching voting age he deliberately voted against the proprietor of the hardware store who was running on his party's ticket. He described the candidate, who had treated him unkindly as a boy, as a "frigid man with a frostbitten ego." Naylor had sold the man scrap iron for a few pennies, and when he approached him in the store he was rebuffed in icy tones, "as if the diminutive urchin was guilty of a piece of unpardonable impertinence."

Pausing to gaze at a knife in a showcase, he had asked, "How-how much is that big knife in there?"

The storekeeper replied irritably, "Oh, get out—get on out! You haven't got money enough to buy that knife. Get on out."[212]

Young Naylor rushed out, his lips tremulous and his eyes moist with tears of mortification. He recalled that bitterness and found satisfaction at the ballot box. In relating the incident years afterward, Naylor failed to note whether the man won or lost; evidently what mattered was that his vote had evened a personal score.

Naylor, like his stepfather, was a staunch Republican, but he did not hesitate to cross party lines and vote on principle. Because of this, he once was called "he with the political coat of many colors."[213] In 1896 he bolted the Republican party and ran for the Ohio state legislature on the Free Silver ticket. Before 1873, the term "Free Silver" meant that no additional fees were imposed on those who brought silver to the mint in exchange for silver dollars. But when the price of silver exceeded the mint price of $1.29 per ounce, very little silver made it to the mint. Consequently, few silver dollars were in circulation when Congress passed the Coinage Act of 1873. No provision was made in the act for the coinage of silver, thus unofficially putting the country on a gold standard. The country was already in a deflationary downward spiral that would last until 1896. Prices had plunged fifty percent, hitting debt-ridden farmers in the west and south especially hard. Silver prices slipped to sixty-five cents an ounce by 1895. The proponents of Free Silver were certain that the return to free and unlimited coinage of silver would raise prices and reduce the burden of debt. Farmers supported the movement that brought them so much hope.

A zealous supporter of William Jennings Bryan, who was a fierce advocate of Free Silver, Naylor embraced Bryan's theory in a run for the Ohio State Senate in 1896. Naylor lost the election, as did Bryan. Although disappointed, he enjoyed the entire process, and the challenge was irresistible.

Naylor undoubtedly heard Bryan speak somewhere in Ohio while Bryan was campaigning as the Democratic candidate for president in 1896. One of the most popular orators in American history, Bryan used his voice to his advantage, particularly when he took his campaign by train directly to the people, giving hundreds of speeches in towns across the U.S. Naylor would have listened very carefully, not just to Bryan's wonderful rhetoric, but to his use of inflection, phrasing, and emphasis in expressing himself so well.

Howard White, a contemporary of Naylor's, recalled the 1896 election in what he called the "days of oratory." Orators often asked rhetorical questions just for emphasis, not expecting an answer.

"There was a fellow speaking in the opera house," White said, motioning across the river to McConnelsville, "and he asked one of those questions. And Jim Naylor was sitting way up among the rafters in the balcony.

"The speaker didn't expect an answer. But Jim Naylor answered him. And the answer Jim gave was not the answer this fellow wanted. Jim told him. The speaker passed it off by saying: 'Well, I guess you're on the wrong side.'"[214]

In August, 1897, Naylor, an eager and enthusiastic candidate, was nominated by the Democrats for state representative, but once again he lost.[215] Two years later, in 1899, Naylor was once again chosen to run on the Democratic ticket, this time in a local school board election that was said to have generated much bitterness. He was criticized by the local press and supposedly lost by a landslide.[216]

Gregarious and intelligent, Naylor loved to argue politics, the weather, or any other topic, especially when he visited the barbershop in Malta for a shave each day at about the same time, knowing that some of his cronies would be there. He could be counted upon to bring up a controversial subject and if, by chance, most agreed with him, he would take the opposite side for the sake of argument. These sessions often ended with Naylor departing wearing a smug grin while his friends were cussing him. One of his cronies said that "fooling with Naylor in a debate was like monkeying with a buzz saw."[217]

Because of his deep-seated interest and participation in Ohio politics, he knew many of the party leaders quite well and developed more than a passing friendship with some of them, including Warren G. Harding. Harding, just five years younger than Naylor, had acquired the *Marion Star* with the financial help of his father in 1884. Within a few years, the daily newspaper was prospering and Harding had become a successful businessman. Over the ensuing years, Harding wrote thousands of thought-provoking editorials about local, state, and national issues on subjects that were of special interest to Naylor.

By the campaign of 1896, Harding had become well known as he traveled throughout the state speaking on behalf of William McKinley, the successful Republican candidate for President who defeated Bryan. In 1899, at the age of thirty-three, Harding ran for the Ohio Senate in a district that had been solidly Democratic, and he won. Harding was well regarded by party leaders for his ability to solve legislative problems. In 1904, with their support, he was elected Ohio's lieutenant governor. In that capacity he made frequent political speeches throughout Ohio, and he went on to become one of the most popular speakers on the Chautauqua circuit as well.[218] Somewhere early in Harding's career, Harding and Naylor became acquainted.

In 1910, Naylor was again persuaded to enter the political arena, but he was defeated in the spring primary in his bid for the nomination for state representative. At that time he said, "I'll never run for office again—unless I take the notion."[219] Just a few months later, in the fall of 1910, he did take the "notion" and ran for the Ohio State Senate in the Ninth-Fourteenth district.[220] This time Naylor was a candidate on the same ticket as Harding, who was then running for governor of Ohio. They frequently appeared at the same places at the same time, cementing their relationship into a warm friendship.

Figure 10.1 - Naylor for Senate in 1910. Courtesy of Greg and Ellen Hill.

One Naylor campaign address that is well remembered was delivered to a crowd of listeners during a debate of issues at Smith Chapel in Centre Township, Morgan County. In a rip-roaring speech he spoke with great emphasis, holding the audience spellbound. His opponent, a poor speaker, lacked color and was a sorry spectacle when he appeared after Naylor. Naylor's "sarcasm, ready tongue, and keen wit were devastating in the rough and tumble of political debate."[221]

Harding lost his bid for governor, and, once again, Naylor lost, but not by very much. According to the official election results, Naylor received nearly 47 percent of the 35,822 votes. The Democratic winner, Chris McKee garnered 48 percent, winning by 478 votes. F. C. Stumpf, a candidate on the Socialist ticket, won 1,562 votes, while W. B. Barnett, the Prohibition candidate, won 356. In Morgan County, Naylor beat his opponent 1,988 to 1,746. He made his best showing in Athens County, winning 4,141 to his opponent's 2,556.[222]

A number of his admirers were glad that he did not win. One wrote, "Ah, doctor, you made a narrow escape. Give thanks for those few votes that defeated you and that keep you sweet and clean as our poet laureate."[223] Naylor did not run for political office again, although he participated in local politics, serving as a member of the Malta town council, the school board, and the board of health at various times.[224]

Writing about Politics

Naylor was passionate about everything in his life, and politics was no exception. That he would combine his love of poetry with his passion for politics was not surprising. His earliest poem of political significance appeared prior to 1900 while he was still using S. Q. Lapius as his pen name. "Call the Roll" dealt with the sudden disappearance of the names of a number of Democratic Congressmen from the House. He seldom wrote political items under his pseudonym, but in this case he did, and an editor commented that it was "ably written" and "showed that the author was well versed in the characteristics of public men."[225] The poem was reprinted in a number of newspapers, and an article written some months later indicated that it was going the rounds of the press without credit to Naylor. It had appeared in a number of papers as original material.[226]

By 1907, Naylor was writing more and more political poetry. He was shrewd in his assessment of many politicians. In a series of political poems, "Who's You—In Ohio," he presented colorful descriptions of various politicians that were either favorable or critical according to his judgment. Included in this series of poems were "Charles Hungry Grosvenor," "George Boss Cox," "Joseph Beensome Foraker," and

"Nickle-Us Longworth." The articles, illustrated by his friend, Westerman, were widely applauded and, in some instances, provided welcome assistance to a favored candidate. Sometimes Naylor voiced his estimate in satirical terms; and his comparisons were often sharp, especially when he contrasted the candidate with Theodore Roosevelt, one of his heroes. In promoting the Naylor-Westerman commentaries, the *Ohio State Journal* received frequent bitter responses from those who had been depicted in an uncomplimentary manner.

Following his 1910 defeat, Naylor mailed to those patients who owed on their accounts a charming poem titled "A Plea and a Promise." In it, he promised to leave the political arena, admitted his dire financial situation and, in a most pleasant manner, asked them all to pay.

> Election day has come and gone—
>   And gone, too, are my hopes;
> For Fate gave me a final punch—
>   And knocked me through the ropes.
> My chances and my pocketbook
>   Together went to smash;
> And so I'm out of politics—
>   And, also, out of cash.
> Old Winter's knocking at my door;
>   And in the dismal dawn
> He whistles through the keyhole: "Son,
>   Where has all your money gone?"
> And when I open not to him,
>   He rattles at my sash
> And shrieks: "Your bills are overdue;
>   You've got to raise some cash!"
> Kind friend, if you will come around
>   And pay your meager score,
> I pledge my word to you I'll be
>   A candidate no more.
> My head has felt the fist of Fate,
>   My back, Misfortune's lash;
> I need your sympathy, good friend—

> Likewise, I need your cash.
> From this day forth I'll minister
> Unto my neighbor's ills,
> Nor meddle much with politics—
> I'll simply pedal pills;
> I'll try to serve all faithfully—
> This is no promise rash.
> So come around and shake my hand—
> And leave a little cash.[227]

After the 1910 November election Naylor admitted that the "notion" had cured him. He declared himself immune. "I know when I—and the people—have had more than enough. But like the canned dog, I've still got a few howls and yelps left in me..." he said.[228]

And howl he did in a lengthy article that appeared in a McConnelsville newspaper shortly after the election, prefaced with the words, "This article is semi-humorous, semi-barbarous."[229] The Republicans were swept out of office, and Naylor wrote, "Evidently the people set in to clean house—and ended by tearing the edifice down.... There's nothing left of the house of republicanism but the blackened hearth stone and the leg chains of the elephant."[230]

According to Naylor, there was no making sense of the election. The issue of temperance and prohibition was a case in point. Just a year or two previously, the four counties north of Morgan County voted overwhelmingly dry. In this election, they defeated one dry candidate for state senator and almost defeated the other. He said, "Electing wet men to maintain and enforce dry legislation is like sending the devil as a revivalist to build up a backslidden church."[231] Yet he claimed, "I'm not wholly disgruntled and discouraged—not at all.... So far as I'm concerned, I'll never do another aerobatic stunt in the sawdust arena. The life's too strenuous for yours sincerely; and I seem to be a little stiff in the joints, anyhow."[232]

Naylor wrote the words to quite a number of campaign songs for the Republican Glee Club. He was a long-time member of the club that was organized in 1872 in Columbus, Ohio, to participate in the presidential campaign of Ulysses S. Grant. The club marched in parades and sang at political events. In campaigns that followed, the club adopted the names of the presidential candidate.[233] The oldest political Glee Club in the country, it boasted top caliber leaders and conductors and had a large membership that seldom fell below seventy-five or eighty, and climbed during presidential campaigns to one hundred eighty or more. In an era long before electronic media and devices, members lifted their voices in "all kinds of music from the highest operatic and oratorio selections down to the commonest ballads, street songs and ragtime. It has given all kinds of entertainment—music could be made a feature from operas to concerts, minstrel shows, vaudeville, and all kinds of combinations of each."[234]

Naylor rewrote the words to quite a number of catchy and popular tunes of the day, and these were included in the group's various books of campaign songs.[235] In June 1916, he attended the annual Republican Glee Club banquet in Columbus. Harry Daugherty, then a Republican party official, was the toastmaster, Myron T. Herrick, Ohio Governor from 1904 to 1906 and U.S. Ambassador to France from 1912 to 1914, was the principal speaker, and Naylor was "funmaker."[236] When called upon to

Figure 10.2 - Republican Glee Club Banquet (inset of Naylor). Courtesy of Robert Naylor.

recite his original verse, "the audience, which had been generous with its applause throughout the evening, gave its greatest measure of praise to Naylor."[237] Shortly afterward he was asked to write more campaign songs and was invited to the Chicago convention as a guest of the Glee Club. At the convention, he "arose to flights of oratory with a well-seasoned and emotional appeal which, had it been delivered in any of the great gathering halls of the nation, would have stamped the speaker with platform immortality."[238]

For the next presidential campaign in 1920, he was again deeply involved. In August he commented, "I'm nearly 'busting' myself writing campaign songs."[239] By mid-August he had mailed fifteen campaign songs to the Glee Club, and on August 30, 1920, he attended a meeting of the Harding Club in Columbus where The Glee Club sang his songs.[240]

Expressing his Political Opinions

Naylor's stint as a newspaper columnist was one of his most lucrative ventures, and it can be attributed directly to his close association with Harding. Both men retreated from politics for a while after their defeat in the 1910 election. At the end of 1912, the *Ohio Star* was launched as a state publication and party periodical. A group of Republican party leaders sought to bring republicans in Ohio closer together by taking over the *Marion Weekly Star* at Marion. Warren Harding was responsible for overall editorial supervision, Naylor was the literary editor, and Dr. Clarence Maris of Columbus, the official publicity man for the state party for more than twelve years, was the managing editor and photographer. Their goal was to convince the people of the state that real reform could be obtained only through the republican party.[241]

Naylor's first column as literary editor appeared in the *Ohio Star* in January, 1913, titled "Sunshine Corner." According to his introductory article, the *Ohio Star* was to be an independent paper with ideas and ideals that he said would be held to tenaciously. It had principles and opinions that they would promulgate boldly and fearlessly. Naylor chose to use the personal pronoun in all his signed articles, "because he desires to stand personally responsible for every statement he makes, every opinion he expresses, every conclusion he draws."[242]

Theodore Roosevelt chose not to run for reelection after his first full term in office ended in 1909, leaving the party divided between conservatives and progressives wanting reform. Roosevelt supported William Howard Taft in his bid for the presidency in 1908, but Taft was not as politically astute as his predecessor, and he was unable to find a common ground between the two factions. As loyal party members, Harding and Naylor could not abide Roosevelt's attacks on President Taft, and they were outspoken in their editorials. When Roosevelt could not obtain the party's nomination in 1912, he left the party and ran for a third term on his progressive, "Bull Moose" ticket, opening the door for the election of the Democratic candidate, Woodrow Wilson. Wilson went on to serve a second term, and Harding and Naylor were harshly critical of him.

Harding did not remain out of politics for long. In 1914 he ran for the United States Senate and won easily. Even after the election, he occasionally wrote for the *Ohio Star*, and his association and friendship with Naylor continued. The following year, Naylor began writing a daily column for the *Marion Star*, "Life's Vaudeville," a column that continued under his byline for eight years. While Naylor's subject matter was often diverse, many columns were politically oriented, particularly during campaigns.

Well-read, Naylor kept himself informed with a daily perusal of various newspapers that provided a constant source of ideas for his columns. He often mined the editorial pages of other newspapers for material that he could use in his column. In one instance in 1916, J. A. A. Burnquist, the Republican lieutenant governor of Minnesota succeeded to governor upon the death of Winfield Hammond, the Democratic governor, and he refused to turn out the former governor's appointees to put in his own. An editorial by someone else in a Democratic daily in Columbus approved of the actions of the new governor because "where the party was serving the country well it was fulfilling its purpose and should not be disturbed." Naylor saw this as a "sly dig at the jolly ribs" of Frank B. Willis, the Republican governor of Ohio who "smashed the carefully constructed Democratic machine—left him by Cox, just as the voters of the state instructed him to do; and now Democratic politicians are displeased with him and peeved at him—naturally." According to Naylor, those Ohio Democrats in appointed positions sought to "hamper, hinder and bedevil" Willis in every way possible. Because they thought that they were secure in their jobs, they could cause Willis' administration to fail. Naylor added, referring to the Democrats, "They forget, however, that they have done in national administration just what Governor Willis has done in state administration. But of course that's a piebald mule of another color."[243]

The editor of the *Ohio State Journal* called Bainbridge Colby, President Wilson's selection for a new secretary of state in 1920, "a complete surprise and a pleasant one" because he felt that the president had gotten away from "the spirit of narrow partisanship" that had marked his administration's choices in important appointments.[244]

Naylor was quite blunt in his response, by asking "of what party was he thinking? He had not the Democratic party in mind, surely; for these men were not Democrats. They were Socialists. Is President Wilson really a Socialist?" Rather, Naylor continued, "...isn't he just favoring his personal favorites, his personal adherents—no matter their politics, or fitness for the positions to which he appoints them? Isn't he just paying political debts—and bargaining for future support?"[245]

The editor also said, "Mr. Colby is now classified as a Republican, but he was a great supporter of Colonel Roosevelt, a Progressive of the Progressives." Ever the staunch Republican, Naylor responded by writing, "Who classifies Mr. Colby as a Republican? I want to know. He may have been a follower of Theodore Roosevelt, at one time. But such a follower! A follower who readily and rapidly forgot all the teachings of the great American—and followed Wilson, as the leader 'kept us out of war.' Bah! Such talk makes me sick of soul. Mr. Colby is simply a political time-server."[246]

The *Journal* editor called Colby "a man of fine character and attainments" and went on to say that "As secretary of state he will not be a rubber stamp." And Naylor responded: "Maybe so—maybe so! But if Mr. Colby is all that the Journal man asserts he is—well, he won't hold his position long. No such man as that can stay long in President Wilson's cabinet. President Wilson is a collector of rubber stamps."[247]

But Colby did indeed hold his position in Wilson's cabinet and went on to become a partner in Wilson's law firm after he left office.[248]

In the 1916 elections, both presidential candidates avoided the issue of prohibition because both wet and dry factions were part of their constituencies and neither wanted to alienate them in what would be a close election. The 18th Amendment to the constitution, approved in 1917 and ratified early in 1919, banned the manufacture, sale, transportation, and import and export of alcohol. The amendment left it to Congress and the states to do the enforcing. The result of their legislative decision was The National Prohibition Act.

The definition of an alcoholic beverage as measured by its alcoholic content was of major concern. The act defined anything above 0.05 percent as intoxicating. President Wilson felt that people would be more willing to give up hard liquor if beer was still an option. He thought the act too severe and vetoed it. Congress, determined to demand a total ban, overrode Wilson's veto.[249] When the Prohibition Enforcement Measure passed over Wilson's veto, Naylor commented, "One more crack in the plaster paris saint."[250] He might have relished Wilson's defeat, but he was not necessarily for prohibition.

In another column, Naylor relied on satire to get his point across. He defended mine workers who went on strike because the manager of the mine discharged three men for willful negligence in endangering their lives and the lives of other miners. Naylor commented:

> Such meddlesome influence deserves the heartiest condemnation of all right-thinking people. The idea of an American employer interfering with the American employee's inalienable right and inestimable privilege of getting killed as often as he pleases—and endangering the lives of his fellows as frequently as he likes! Who ever heard of such open arrogance and shameless tyranny!...What's this country coming to anyhow? If employers insist on giving attention to the safety and welfare of their employees, one of the chief subjects of demagogic oratory will be obliterated—a consummation devoutly to be deplored."[251]

JAMES BALL NAYLOR

Naylor was compelled to share his personal beliefs in his columns. He was very outspoken in one column responding to an article in *The Industrial Worker* of Spokane, whom he called "an organ of the I.W.W." The Industrial Workers of the World, an international union, reached its peak in the early 1920s. Its goal, then and now, is to unite all workers within a single union as a class and abolish the wage system entirely.

Naylor felt that the article, although ostensibly against sabotage, actually suggested its employment. He stated: "I don't believe in abridging the freedom of speech or the freedom of the press; but I do believe in suppressing incendiary individuals or publications that slyly advise in favor of violation of the law—destruction of property and possible loss of life." He went on to say, "Liberty and license are not related; every American should be granted the fullest liberty under the law, but no person should be granted the slightest license beyond the law. And the man who advises the commission of a crime is as guilty as the man who commits the crime."[252]

While many of his columns were politically motivated, others were often light, whimsical pieces or on subjects that offended his sense of social justice. His wit and marvelous sense of humor were readily apparent. Naylor took exception to an editorial in *Collier's Weekly* deriding Andrew Carnegie's generosity in proposing to pension ex-presidents. Naylor personally did not agree, but he defended Carnegie's right to dispose of his money as he saw fit and pointed out that the more Carnegie disposed of that way, the more money would be returned to circulation, benefiting the entire country. He added sarcastically, "Perhaps, though, the mistake Mr. Carnegie has made is that he hasn't offered to pension ex-editors."[253]

Naylor's critical attitude toward organized religion sometimes surfaced in his columns. A bishop's statement given in an address at Savannah, Georgia, caused him to react with annoyance. The bishop said, "Rome in its worst days never harbored such conditions of vice as are prevalent in our highest social circles at the present time."[254]

Naylor replied in an editorial that he presumed the bishop would not make such scathing assertions from hearsay evidence alone; yet if he wished to convey the idea that he spoke from experience, he showed a lack of knowledge of true social ethics to thus tell tales out of school. To do so, Naylor contended, the bishop inadvertently laid himself open to the same attack he made on others.

Naylor felt a simple truth lay at the heart of the whole matter:

> Crime knows all classes; vice visits all grades of society. Money neither makes nor mars morals. Wealth doesn't contaminate; poverty doesn't disinfect. The rich man isn't necessarily a sinner; the poor man isn't necessarily a saint. The division of humanity into classes is an artificial affair, mainly; but considering such division: the upper class has its foibles, the middle class has its faults, and the lower class has its failings.... What's the use of charging 'our highest social circles' with vices and vanities that are common to all grades of society? Is it fair? Is it kind? And what's the use of making such a statement as the good bishop made anyhow? Will it mend matters? No. It will do but one thing—deepen the false impression already too prevalent and too well-marked, that morality is a matter of money—or the lack of money; that good manners and good morals don't go together."[255]

Some of Naylor's observations on contemporary life provide a sharp contrast to the present day.

> Coins are like people—they have their personal habits: the penny carries postcards and goes to Sunday-school; the nickel chews gum and patronizes the picture show; the dime shines shoes and loafs at the barber shop; the quarter wears Paris garters and reads the Smart Set; the half-dollar buys a red necktie—and goes to the circus; and the dollar—ah! the dollar is the all-around coin, the true cosmopolite; has all kinds of habits, is all things to all men, is popular in all society and welcome in all walks of life.[256]

Occasionally in his columns, he wrote warm human interest pieces, such as "One Woman, One Wagon, and One Horse" about Mary Titcomb of Washington County, Maryland, who loaded a little wagon with books from the Hagerstown library. She took them over the steep and rough roads into the mountains where she circulated the books among the people there who would not or could not come to the library in town. One sad day her wagon was destroyed when it was hit by a train. The townspeople provided her with a motor car so she could continue her work. According to Naylor, for the first six months of 1912 more than 28,000 books were circulated to schools and homes in the county.[257]

Naylor received his share of fan mail that occasionally included a letter or two from an oddball. He received one asking him to write an essay for a contest since he was so good at it. Naylor obliged with the following, "Success frequently comes from an admixture of unmitigated gall and unmodified rascality, the said admixture enabling the possessor to feast upon the fruits of the other fellow's toil and genius."[258]

Being a Critical and Supportive Patriot

Naylor was an unrelenting critic of Wilson's policies, particularly his strict policy of neutrality before World War I, yet once the U.S. was embroiled in the war, he was a staunch supporter and patriot. Naylor admired and supported Charles Evans Hughes, an associate justice of the Supreme Court and former governor of New York, who was the Republican candidate in the 1916 presidential campaign against Wilson. Neither a liberal nor a conservative, considered capable and honest, Hughes nevertheless antagonized the Old Guard Republican financial interests. Elihu Root, Roosevelt's Secretary of State in 1905 and senator from New York in 1909 to 1915, was the Old Guard's choice for the Republican presidential nomination. Hughes' candidacy was the result of a compromise at last between the conservative and progressive wings of the party. Hughes was critical of Wilson, but he failed to provide alternatives to Wilson's policies and lost the election.[259]

With Europe in turmoil, Wilson campaigned on a policy of strict neutrality. The U.S. had strong ties with Britain and France, but Wilson was concerned because of the large number of immigrants from Austria and Germany. His campaign slogan was "He Kept Us Out of War."

In 1915, when the unarmed British liner Lusitania was torpedoed by a German submarine and sunk with the loss of nearly 1,200 lives, including 124 Americans, Wilson argued, "There is such a thing as a man too proud to fight."[260] Naylor was especially dismayed because his good friend, Elbert Hubbard, and his wife lost their lives on the Lusitania when it went down.

Naylor was distressed over the dangerous situation and the expanding war in Europe, and he expressed himself with considerable fervor, "Oh, for a Roosevelt in the presidential chair."[261] Because he was an active voice in Ohio politics, the Republican Committee in Noble County urged him to campaign for them in October, 1916. He conveyed his concerns to Ohio party leaders Governor Willis, former Governor Herrick, and Harding about the political outlook.

Early in 1917, with the war raging in Europe, the United States could no longer remain neutral. President Wilson asked a special session of Congress to declare war on the government of Germany. Four days later Congress passed a formal declaration of war against Germany and entered the war three years after it had actually begun and fought in it for just over a year. Wilson introduced a new income tax to help pay for the war, amounting to almost $16.5 billion, half of what was spent on the war. Liberty Bond drives provided the remainder of the money.[262]

At fifty-six, Naylor was too old to fight in World War I, but his age did not keep him from participating on the home front. Naylor was actively involved in patriotic support of the conflict. He made countless appearances throughout Morgan and surrounding counties and often, after a hard day's work, he traveled long distances to fulfill an engagement. Whenever requested, he spoke about the issues facing the nation and the problems of the servicemen. No worthy cause was denied his wholehearted support. Throughout the war he gave literally hundreds of speeches at YMCAs and Red Cross meetings as he campaigned in support of Liberty bond drives.

Poems written during this period were mostly patriotic in nature. He printed a number of short ones on post cards and giveaway cards that he sold to banks and other businesses where they were distributed to

Figure 10.3 - Malta Depot during World War I. Courtesy of *The Morgan County Herald*.

customers. In April 1917, his poem "Old Glory" was printed on letter-sized paper for sale and distribution, and he noted in his diary that he had sold 4,000 in Malta alone. All the money was contributed to the Red Cross and other organizations that supported the war effort.

Many times during the war years, Naylor presented his lengthy lecture, "One Country, One People, One Flag," and delivered it with an enthusiasm that always aroused a patriotic response. Taking his audience on a journey through history, beginning in the Garden of Eden, Naylor tells of a continued story of war right up to World War I, touching on the Revolutionary War, the Civil War, the Spanish-American War, and the Philippine-American War. Interspersed among his oratory were a number of his poems, such as "Cuba Libre," "A Millionaire Dude," "Razzer Jim," "A Typical Yankee Boy," "Follerin' The Fife An' Drum," and others.

Naylor made himself available whenever a group of young men left to join the armed forces, always sending them off with a rousing speech. He was on hand to see his own son depart. Robert was wounded in

Europe, and on November 3, 1918, First Sergeant Bob Naylor wrote his parents, "I have been in an Australian hospital here in Belgium for some weeks. I went to the hospital for shrapnel wounds in the right hand. I received the wound in the last big drive, around Ghent."[263]

Naylor followed the war news closely, and was in complete disagreement with Wilson, whom he considered incompetent. Distressed with the progress of events, he worried about his son. Robert wrote regularly, but the mail was often slow, which upset Naylor. He was now having frequent annoying bouts with personal ailments that added to the stress. He admitted that "anxiety, like an acid, etches sorrow in the soul."[264]

Naylor criticized Wilson for his attitude of "peace at any price" in settling a railroad trainmen's strike that the author felt encouraged further labor disruptions. It was not long before the streetcar workers went on strike in New York, followed by steel workers and coal miners. When he learned that coal miners in a neighboring county threatened to strike, he drove over to the mine to talk to them. The miners were in an ugly mood, but Naylor courageously gave a forceful talk, telling them plainly that if they went on strike they would be working for the enemy and would be traitors to their own country. He did not retreat in his choice of words in the face of their antagonism and, when he had finished, the miners applauded him vigorously and returned to work.

When Theodore Roosevelt died in January, 1919, the complexion of the 1920 Republican presidential nomination was changed. The Republicans were in control of the United States Senate, and Harding was on the Senate's Foreign Relations Committee and positioning himself as a potential candidate. When President Wilson spoke in Columbus, Ohio, about his proposed League of Nations, he accused the Senate of holding up approval of the treaty. The speech brought forth a bitter response from Naylor, "...same old glittering generalities, gorgeous platitudes and grinning Mrs. Wilson! Heaven help us!"[265]

Before the final vote, Harding spoke against a proposed reservation to the treaty, one that Republicans knew was unacceptable to Wilson. The reservation was the condition that the United States would not be obliged to defend any other country at the request of the League of Nations without prior Congressional approval.

Naylor was forceful in his opposition to the League of Nations. At the Masonic Lodge he got into a controversy with two other members. Later, when it looked like the Senate would approve the covenant for the League of Nations, Naylor was furious. When the Senate voted on the resolution of ratification, including fourteen reservations, the measure failed by a 39-55 vote. Later the Senate considered a resolution to approve the treaty without any reservations, but it also failed.[266] The Senate's rejection of Wilson's treaty resulted in Naylor voicing his delight, "Glory be! More power to the Republican Senators—loyal and wise Americans!" [267]

Naylor further vocalized his opposition to the League of Nations in a column where he wrote:

> Let's put the following questions forever at rest: Is America going to join the league of nations—at any time, on any condition? She is not! Is America—in any treaty, alliance, or conference—going to sign away a single one of her national rights or privileges? She is not! Some good people are worrying a deal today over whether the present administration, finally, is going to adopt the Wilson foreign policies. These good people may put their minds at rest. The people of America, by an overwhelming majority, told President Harding what they wanted him to do: and he's going to do it.[268]

He continued:

> America, as always, is ready to join with the other civilized powers of earth to do the good work of the world that needs to be done. But America will say what work she is to undertake, when she is to undertake it, and how she is to perform it. America will remain boss of her own soul![269]

Naylor held a very poor estimate of Herbert Hoover, Harding's Secretary of Commerce who succeeded Coolidge in 1929. By then very disillusioned with the Republican Party, he exclaimed bitterly, "Never saw such political chaos in my life; no party leaders; no party lines, no party issues,"[270] but he continued to write about candidates, commenting that "I have been writing bits—and 'obits' for candidates."[271] Hoover's acceptance speech was condemned as "glittering generalities, pyrotechnic platitudes,"[272] and he was particularly bitter because Harding was not mentioned. He felt that Hoover's election, with a Republican Congress "will leave him no excuse for failure."[273] As his discouragement increased, he commented, "Trying to write political editorials is getting on my nerves! Hell; there is no party politics."[274]

Public Service

In 1920, Naylor secured a reasonably lucrative position as District Health Commissioner for Morgan County. For his services he received a salary of $1,500 a year plus expenses.[275] Given the stress and eventual health challenges associated with dabbling in politics while maintaining a full-time medical practice and pursuing his literary career, he was relieved to have the financial stability.

As Health Commissioner he conducted baby clinics, "jag cures" for alcoholics, spoke on health matters, and made inspection trips around the county. He was a paid public servant, but the nature of the work often aroused hostility in people with whom he had to deal. On his inspection trips around the county he diagnosed contagious diseases, and it was sometimes necessary for him to quarantine and fumigate homes and schools. Some of those quarantined, finding themselves inconvenienced, attempted to disregard his orders; but with public welfare his primary concern, Naylor was forced to take steps to ensure that they were obeyed.

While his duty was clear, he was not blind to the hardships that it often caused and was not unsympathetic to the people involved. He acted in what he clearly understood to be the best interest of the public. Collectively they agreed, but individually some who were personally affected expressed anger at his decisions. They interpreted his orders as bureaucratic infringement of their rights.

On February 2, 1920, two days after he accepted the office as Health Commissioner, he issued orders closing down all public meetings because of a flu epidemic. Thirty-five men at the plow factory alone were on the sick list. People were frightened, some refusing to care for those who were ill, an attitude that made Naylor "sick of soul."[276] By the time he lifted the flu ban three weeks later, he had alienated a number of people, one of whom swore he would force Naylor out of office. Outspoken and never one to retreat from an argument or fight, he did not mince words in denouncing those who defied his orders or objected to the way he performed his job.

But for a man more used to satisfied patients and an admiring public, the emotional impact of the unpleasantness distressed him deeply.

The number of contagious cases was incredible, especially of smallpox in Morgan County, and Naylor conscientiously diagnosed each one. These were reported to the State Department of Health where his reports were read with skepticism because of the large numbers. A man was sent to tell him that his smallpox cases were probably chickenpox, but when he checked and they proved to be smallpox, Naylor was vindicated. His ego, however, was badly bruised and his resentment was long lasting.

Disillusionment during the Harding Years

Naylor's reputation within the political community in Ohio was enhanced in June, 1920, when Warren G. Harding was nominated for president. His status as a friend of the President of the United States brought him personal satisfaction and strengthened his position as a political columnist. Harding once told Charles Dawes, Naylor's old schoolmate at Marietta and later vice president under Coolidge, "Dr. Naylor as a campaign orator would be worth $50,000 a year to the Republican National Executive Committee."[277] When Harding was nominated, Naylor wondered, "What changes will it make in my worldly fortunes?"[278]

By the time that Harding had offered him an appointment in the Treasury Department, Naylor was entrenched as Health

Commissioner, and he declined. When he was offered an appointment to the Ohio State Medical Board, he declined again. Both offers meant a move away from Malta. By now sixty years of age and in what he considered declining health, Naylor preferred to remain at Elmhurst. He did, however, solicit a favor on behalf of his son, and a position as a Federal agent under the Treasury Department in Prohibition Enforcement materialized for Robert after Naylor corresponded with George B. Christian, Jr., Secretary to the President. Christian wrote to J. R. Russell, State Prohibition Commissioner:

> Dr. James Ball Naylor, of Malta, Morgan County, one of the most prominent Republicans of that section, is exceedingly desirous of having his son...receive an appointment in your department.
> I may say that Dr. Naylor is a contributor to the editorial page of the Marion Star and that the President is much interested in young Naylor being placed.[279]

Following Harding's inauguration, Naylor was hired to write editorials for the *Chicago Journal of Commerce*, and he began working for the paper under special arrangements, eventually leading to a column, "Life's Infinite Variety."[280] The column appeared during Harding's presidency from April, 1921 to April, 1923. Naylor's long-running daily column in the *Marion Star*, "Life's Vaudeville," continued as well.

Although Naylor supported Harding and his administration without equivocation, he had reason to be disappointed in Harding's lack of party leadership. Congress was overwhelmingly Republican with the largest majority in party history. Of the 435 congressmen in the House, 303 were Republicans. Ninety of these were first term congressmen. In the Senate, of the ninety-six senators, fifty-nine were Republicans, yet the party was less effective than before. Harding did not consider it his role as President to push his program through Congress. Instead he left it to the party leadership, but they were not up to the challenge.

JAMES BALL NAYLOR

Naylor was unable to be completely objective because many of the politicians involved were personal friends, and his articles no doubt reflected a biased attitude. At the end of March, 1923, probably because of his unswerving loyalty to Harding, the *Chicago Journal of Commerce* cut Naylor's article, and within two weeks they notified him that he was dropped from the staff. This was particularly worrisome, because in January, with his position as Health Commissioner reasonably secure, he sold his practice and equipment to Dr. H. Humphrey. In July, 1923, Harding was stricken in San Francisco first with food poisoning, then with pneumonia. Naylor immediately expressed his concern. Upon Harding's death a few days later he wrote, "The country has lost a great President. I have lost a good friend."[281] Two days later at Chautauqua memorial services in McConnelsville he spoke for the late president. Six weeks later, barely a month after he purchased a new Willys-Knight sport car, "the turbid flood of ill luck" saw him dropped from the staff of the *Marion Star*.[282]

In June, 1924, Charles Dawes, who gained a prominent role in Harding's administration as the first director of the Bureau of the Budget and saved the country more than a billion dollars with his business acumen and principles of economy and efficiency, spoke in Malta during his campaign for vice president. Naylor was on hand to introduce him.[283] It was not long before he was again "writing some stuff for the Republican National Committee."[284] His spirits improved, and the material he sent the committee was, in his own words, "a taste of real Republicanism—peppered with a little hell."[285]

Although Naylor continued to be involved in politics, speaking at political meetings throughout the state, he was often disheartened by what was happening in Washington. He makes no mention in his diaries of the scandals that emerged, beginning with the Teapot Dome scandal shortly after Harding's death. Albert Fall, Harding's close friend from his days in the Ohio Senate and his Secretary of the Interior, had negotiated leases with private oil companies, an action that outraged conservationists. Many questions were raised in the Senate hearings that followed, but the one that drew blood had to do with Fall's sudden prosperity after a period of financial difficulties.

Because Daugherty was still heading the Department of Justice, his impartiality was challenged, and he was forced to resign. More investigations followed, often accompanied by sensational public hearings that produced a decade of civil and criminal proceedings. Daugherty, despite the investigations that followed, was never convicted, but that did not prove he was innocent. Harding was never implicated in any explicit wrongdoing, but he was blamed for choosing the men who did do wrong.

A month after Harding's death, Naylor responded to an editorial in the *Zanesville Signal*:

> This editorial statement is a studied effort to make those who loved our dear departed president, and who today revere his memory, believe that he favored America's entrance into the league of nations; and the statement is false—unqualifiedly false. No act of President Harding, no word of his, no suggestion of his, ever contemplated America's entrance into the league of nations; and well this editor knows the truth. But for partisan purposes, he would deliberately misrepresent the purpose and aims of him who today can not speak for himself.[286]

Less than six months after Harding's death it was reported that his wife had burned all of his papers to protect his memory. She was more concerned with concealing a scandal about his personal life, his affair with Carrie Phillips that ended before he became president. Without Harding's papers available to set the record straight, journalists and writers felt free to trash Harding, while those who knew otherwise remained silent, perhaps afraid that their own reputations would be tarnished by association.

Although Naylor gave his full support to Harding and dwelled on all the good that was done by his administration, he felt the brunt of the continuing onslaught of negative press in his own pocketbook when he lost his newspaper jobs because of it. He tried unsuccessfully for more than two years to find another newspaper for which to write and, in a moment of despair he wrote, "Life's grim futility breaks the spirit at last, then the reserve stock of grit becomes exhausted; and— What's the Use!"[287]

His poem "What's the Use," plainly reveals his growing disaapointment and disenchantment:

> A daily fight, a war of years!
> And wounds, and scars, and toil and tears—
> Bald scheme and ruse!
> To earn a place, to gain a name—
> A foretaste of to-morrow's fame!
>   Ah, what's the use!
>
> A dusty book of verse or plays,
> A grinning skull—the world's mad praise,
> Or vain abuse!
> A withered bit of faded bay—
> Forgotten fame of yesterday!
>   And what's the use!

Figure 10.4 - Naylor's Bookplate. Courtesy of Robert Naylor.

Theresa Marie Flaherty

11
The Last Years

In 1925, Naylor began writing editorials for *The Week* and continued writing for them for the next three years. He was also actively involved with the Republican Executive Committee, yet he was becoming increasingly embittered. He wrote, "Great political campaign in Morgan County; a Republican Executive Committee that knows no more of politics than a pig knows of paradise."[288] Four days later he again commented, "Grand Republican fizzle at the opera house...no crowd, no enthusiasm."[289] On election day he expressed his disappointment, "...gross mismanagement on the part of Republicans—state and local; general hell."[290]

Someone once asked Naylor's old friends at the barbershop in Malta if he ever lost his vigor. Charley Hoops, the barber, exploded, "Did he ever lose his vigor? No sir, you didn't dare say anything against President Harding or Harry Daugherty when Doc was here. He'd come right out of the chair and want to fight you."[291]

In 1926, Naylor was persuaded to write a series of articles for the *Morgan County Herald*, "The Physicians of Morgan County," based on biographical sketches appearing in an 1886 history of the county that included his name as a new physician. Personal recollections of his fellow doctors added spice to the historical series and provided insight into the man himself.

Poetry remained Naylor's first love throughout his lifetime, and he spent considerable time over a number of years planning and preparing another book of verse. Of the more than eight hundred poems that he wrote, less than one hundred fifty appeared in his first four volumes, *Current Coins, Golden Rod and Thistle Down, Old Home Week,* and *Songs From the Heart of Things.* Although he tried to find a publisher for one last volume, his efforts were in vain.

Personal health problems troubling Naylor were aggravated from years of pressure and diversified activity. The harassment he suffered as Health Commissioner, as well as incidents in his own personal life, continued to affect his health. He lost weight. His health declined steadily. Lines were etched deeply into his face as he suffered with bouts of neuritis. Naylor expressed fear in his diary that "some attack will be the last one, but I say nothing to worry the others."[292]

Writing was the one activity that could revive his spirits. In 1927, W. D. Matson, the editor of the *Herald,* asked Naylor to do another series about life in Morgan County, and it was one task that Naylor did enjoy immensely. He said, "It has been said it is a sure sign of age, to begin to indulge in reminiscences. If so-then I've ALWAYS been old; for I've always enjoyed looking back along the road of life—and noting, and remarking upon, my experiences."[293]

The result was *Rambling Reminiscences.* Much of interest about his early life and events in the area, particularly about the 1860's and 1870's, was included. After its appearance in the newspaper, it was published by the *Herald* as a booklet similar to *From Jim to Jack.* Many comparisons can be made of places and incidents described in these two autobiographical works of Naylor.

The following year, Naylor was bitten by a dog and became violently ill from the series of anti-rabies shots that he was required to take. He was bedridden for a month. Because he did not want others to suffer a similar fate, as Health Commissioner, he was harsh in dealing with those who let their dogs run loose. If steps were not taken by owners to protect their own animals, they suffered the consequences. When he ordered stray dogs killed, dog owners responded angrily. His answer: "Let the heathen rage!"[294]

While he was recovering, his old friend Rufus Dawes visited him in Malta. In an interview with Norris Schneider of the *Zanesville Times Signal* many years later, Naylor spoke of their friendship:

Dr. Naylor said: "I want you to know what Ruf did for me a few years ago. All my books were out of print because of fire and bankruptcy of the publishers. My income was cut off and my days of writing were over when he came to my rescue."

The doctor related that he was in Chicago several years ago on a visit when his old friend said, "Jim, why don't you get out a collected edition of your poems, so we can have them all together?"

Dr. Naylor replied that he could not afford it, whereupon his old friend declared: "Well, I made more money than I need this year, and I'll publish the edition."

"No, you don't," Naylor objected. "Poetry does not pay and I don't want anyone to sink his money in a product of mine."

But the brother of former Vice President Charles Dawes of "Hell and Maria" fame, won the argument by asserting explosively, "Damn it, its my money. Can't I do what I please with it?"

The book called *A Book of Buckeye Verse* was published at Rufus Dawes' expense, and thus the pupil repaid his tutor.[295]

After Naylor sent Dawes a manuscript with 262 poems, the galley proofs came, then the page proofs. He received samples of paper and binding cloth from which to choose. When the book was complete, he received copies of the book to sell. Dawes presented Naylor with a copy of the book inscribed:

Dr. James Ball Naylor

I present this book to you, and in doing so derive a pleasure similar to, but of less intensity than that which must fill your heart, when you contemplate your great gift hereby extended to your fellow men.

Rufus C. Dawes – November 22, 1927.[296]

After sending Dawes $250 for the wholesale cost of the books, Dawes wrote that he had received enough, Naylor should keep the rest. Naylor was overwhelmed by the generosity of his friend.[297] Yet there was still an element of disappointment. The book did not come close to being a "complete collection" of his poetry. Nearly half of the poems appeared in his other books, and the rest amounted to a fraction of what he might have wished to include. Without financial resources to do it himself, with no contract, nothing in writing between him and Dawes, he was in no position to make demands, nor did he wish to. Finding himself in such an awkward position was troubling and difficult for a man who was used to being in control of every step in the process.

In 1931, at the age of seventy, after thirteen difficult and demanding years as Health Commissioner, Naylor finally retired.

A Devastating Blow

Late on the stormy New Year's Eve ushering in 1934, Winston and Weston Doty, Naylor's inseparable twenty-year-old twin grandsons, escorted two young ladies to a friend's party in Montrose, California. Well known by thousands as yell leaders at University of Southern California football games, the twins were handsome and bright. They were also thoughtful and loving sons. In the midst of the celebration, at twenty minutes after midnight, they phoned their mother, Olive, in a festive mood and wished her a happy new year.

Later, above the din of music, laughter, and animated voices inside the house, the clamorous sounds of the storm intruded. Fascinated by the awesome display, the twins, their dates, and other friends crowded outside together on the back porch. Mesmerized, they watched a flash flood roar through the almost dry riverbed. Minutes later, a sudden cloudburst unleashed a raging torrent of water that enveloped them, sweeping all but three of the dozen young people to their deaths.[298]

Stripped of protective underbrush by a recent fire, the foothills could not contain the 18-inch rainfall. The water coursed its way into nearby cities, uprooting trees and houses, tearing out bridges, and triggering landslides. The death toll the next day was reported at thirty-nine and the list of missing was at seventy-five and rising. Estimates

Figure 11.1 - Winston and Weston Doty, Naylor's Grandsons. Courtesy of Jean Naylor Finley.

of damages reached into the millions.[299]

The twins' bodies were recovered later. Olive, fearing that the news might be a mortal blow to her parents, arranged for the funeral to be over quickly so that they would be spared the long trip to California. Naylor and his wife were distraught, in disbelief that the twins' lives could be snuffed out when they held so much promise.

Naylor sank deep into a depression, and the family feared that he would not recover from the shock. His diaries from that time were dark and despondent, reflecting his despair. Not wanting him to be remembered in this way, someone in the family destroyed the diaries that covered that period.[300]

Villa, who relied on her faith for consolation in those dark hours, was the solid, sturdy crutch on which her husband could lean. Already in a downward spiral in both mind and body, discouraged from losing his columns, angry over the treatment of Harding, and weakened from his slow and painful recovery from the course of anti-rabies treatment, Naylor was slow to find comfort that would soothe his battered spirit.

When he became disheartened, he often found solace in the outdoors. The beauty of nature awed him, and a walk through the woodlot behind his home helped renew and refresh his spirit. However, for a very long time after the death of the twins, he could find no joy or comfort there.

As he always had, Naylor found comfort in his poetry. His last literary contribution was *Vagrant Verse*, a compilation of forty-six poems that had not been included in any previous book of verse. The collection was published as a pamphlet by *The Morgan County Herald* after appearing in the *Herald* in 1935, more than a year after the death of the twins.

On August 30, 1935, Naylor attended his first meeting of the McConnelsville and Malta Rotary Club as an honorary member, accompanied by his wife, his son Robert, and his daughter Jean. The Rotarians presented him with a gold-headed walking stick engraved in memory of his friendship and in appreciation for his work in leadership matters of human interest and for the inspiration provided by his writings. In a fireside talk with nearly seventy present, Naylor recounted his early experiences in writing and talked of his fellowship with some of the greatest writers of their day, noting their exchange of books and poems and telling humorous anecdotes. One of those present said, "In his talk he assumed a meek, humble spirit of a man modest of his accomplishments. No one within the assemblage felt anything but reverence and exaltation for him as he spoke to them. He is and truly has been a great man among us."[301] To express his appreciation for their thoughtfulness, he presented a copy of *Vagrant Verse* to each of the Rotary Roses present.

Emerging from Despair

One of Naylor's finest moments took place on October 10, 1937 when Marietta College presented him with an honorary degree of Doctor of Literature at the inauguration of Dr. H. K. Eversull as president of the college.[302] In cap and gown, leaning on a cane, Naylor at seventy-seven appears thin and frail.

While the accolades were much welcomed and enjoyed, it seems that he was left wanting, realizing that fame and recognition were

Theresa Marie Flaherty

empty without a purpose in life and someone with whom to share it. Still terribly distraught over the loss of his beloved grandsons, he realized that what mattered most was the comforting warmth and presence of his family and friends and the tender memories of bygone days they shared. One of his friends said:

> His distinquishing traits were honesty of purpose, his intense patriotism, his loyalty to his friends, his concern for the best interest of his family and unswerving appreciation of his beloved wife and the children he had reared. He was a good man, a good husband and father, a good citizen. He lived a life of rectitude and right. He feared no man, nor any circumstance. Like the immortal Lincoln, whom he resembled much in his rise the hard way to eminence among his fellows and in the constancy of devotion to his country, he possessed integrity of character and majesty of conscience. We like this man because he was so human.[303]

Figure 11.2 - Naylor receives Honorary Degree from Marietta College. Courtesy of Lucile Naylor.

Naylor emerged from the depths of despair with a new perspective on living and a greater appreciation for his wife and family and the time they had left. Naylor's days of writing were over, but treasured memories were a measure of consolation. Visitors from throughout the state and beyond often stopped to chat with Malta's famous citizen on their way through the area.

One who knew him well wrote: "He has long since retired from the practice of medicine, being well past 80 years of age. But when we last saw him, a little more than a year

Figure 11.3 - Naylor's family in 1941: Lena, Olive, Robert, Anne, Mrs. Naylor, Jean, Lucile, Dr. Naylor. Courtesy of Greg and Ellen Hill.

ago, he was still 'going strong' at the business of living and enjoying it to the full. We regard him as one of the most interesting characters we've ever encountered."[304]

A wonderful story appeared in print about one such visit to Naylor by a man named Charles Hammon. In 1930, the Russian government purchased the Duber Hamden watch factory at Canton, Ohio, and moved it to Moscow as part of the Bolshevik industrial program. Fifty skilled watchmakers and mechanics accompanied the factory machinery and stayed there for two years to train the workers how to make watches. Among those selected was Hammon. He was often homesick and lonely while in Russia, and he went to the public library searching for something to read in English. There he found *The Kentuckian* and several other novels written by Dr. James Ball Naylor. He eagerly devoured them all more than once. Several years later, on a fishing trip near Malta, he learned that Malta was Naylor's home. A friend arranged a visit to *Elmhurst* so he could express his appreciation. The author of the newspaper article added:

[It] makes us wonder if we have properly appreciated the man of genius who has lived quietly among us all these years and whose works may be found in the four quarters of the globe and which will live after him. Incidentally, what a mighty power is a pen in the hands of a man who can use it. Think of Dr. Naylor living in a small town in Ohio and creating books which may be found on the same shelves with Tolstoi, Turgenieff, Maxim Gorky, Gogol and Dostoyevsky in the public library at Moscow.[305]

In a similar vein, an editor who had recently reread Ralph Marlowe wrote:

Our good Doctor is approaching the three score and ten, and some of these days, in the course of human events, he will 'go the way of all flesh' and with tears in our eyes we will read that delightful poem of his 'Dr. John Goodfellow. Office Upstairs.' To those of us who have lived in the two towns, it has been one of our privileges to have heard him lecture or fearlessly discuss all topics of the day, narrate a story, or visit with him upon the street. It does not occur to most of us, accustomed as we are to seeing the familiar figure of our democratic fellow citizen, that he is a genius—but he is. Few men anywhere have his gift of tongue, his poetic concepts, his descriptive abilities, his inimitable powers of narration and conversation, his keen discernment and his ready and inexhaustible vocabulary with which to paint his word pictures. Dr. Naylor is a striking and a rare character for a small town—and though his life has been spent in the obscure hills of Southeastern Ohio, his literary fame extends from coast to coast. Why do we so often, not maliciously, but thoughtlessly, await until too late to give our flowers?[306]

His death came quietly on April 1, 1945. "His manner of going," said Lucile, "was precisely as he'd have wished it to be—without warning."[307] He had just finished reading Strickland Gillilan's "Finnigan and Flannigan," his favorite humorous poem. He went upstairs to prepare for bed and was stricken with a heart attack.

Although his diverse talents gained him wide recognition elsewhere, Naylor was known especially for his contributions to the literary history of Ohio. His poems, conveying a keen sense of humor and a sympathetic understanding of his fellow men, depicted a contemporary rural Ohio. Its picturesque countryside and its hills and valleys never failed to inspire him. With his pen he created an awareness of the beauty of the Muskingum valley that is undiminished to this day.

His books, for many years out of print, are now in the public domain and have been reprinted since the expiration of his copyrights. Fredonia Books published *The Sign of the Prophet* in 2002 to "make original editions of historical works available to scholars."[308] Other publishers began republishing his books in 2007.[309] Kessinger Publishers has reprinted at least five of Naylor's books in their special Legacy Reprint Series, saying "Because this work is culturally important, we have made it available as part of our commitment to protecting, preserving and promoting the world's literature."[310] Google Books has made most of his novels available for online reading, and reprints of his books are readily available for those who are interested.

Naylor's death evoked glowing tributes, and papers throughout the nation recounted his literary career. A resolution introduced in the 96th General Assembly of the Ohio House of Representatives honored the man "...who a generation ago was perhaps the most outstanding, and certainly the most versatile and prolific man of letters then resident in Ohio."[311]

Although it has not been suggested before, Naylor possessed some of the same attributes that made Will Rogers popular. The pithy, simplistic style that was frank and honest appealed to the public. The Ohio citizens who were never privileged to see or hear the author missed a rare treat, but for many years they came face to face with his remarkable wit and frank opinions in their daily newspapers.

While Naylor was sometimes a controversial figure, he was appreciated by his contemporaries, even in the local community. A tribute by Charles Barrell, one of Naylor's contemporaries in the local community, that appeared in *The Morgan County Herald*, so richly captures how Naylor touched the lives of others in living his own:

> In a big red house on the side of the hill, with its grand old elms, and grander still, lives a fine old codger, with a glint in his eye, with opinions galore, a mind active and spry. He's a sort of tradition, built up by the years, founded on work and joy, on heartaches and tears, an important beacon, and inspiring light, playing hard fighting clean for things that are right. And a sign on the corner will tell you his name, reading, "Dr. Jim Naylor, of national fame." So with a little sarcasm, a good bit of fun, reaching literary heights well worthy of one, climbing step by step, beginning at scratch, stoically, eternally life's problems to match. With a heritage born of struggle and strife, befitting, climaxing a wholesome life. With a light here and there, to brighten the way, a kind word, a rebuke, an impulse to stay the friend or foe, to smooth out the road, to bolster his courage to lighten his load. So, the world's a lot better for his presence here, for his bits of sunshine, for his words of cheer. And his ability to mix up food for our souls, to bright an old world shot full of holes, and it means just one thing, if we know him well, he's human clear through and able to tell in words well put, thinking straight as two strings of the best side of life, "Songs From the Heart of Things." So let's hand him the orchids while we see his smile and not wait 'til we're shocked by the long last mile.[312]

In his lifetime Naylor achieved a measure of greatness that was recognized well beyond the state of Ohio. His legacy is more than the myriad of published material that he left behind; it is a testament to his indomitable spirit and to the moral principles and integrity that defined him. Although he welcomed the acclaim he received, what ultimately mattered most to him were the people he loved and the joy and comfort he brought to others in his role as a physician.

JAMES BALL NAYLOR

NOTES

Chapter 1: The Days of Childhood

1. Richard Walker, Ph. D., "Stockport, Ohio: A Compendium of Historical Information," The Sesquicentennial Committee, Stockport, Ohio, 1984. Stockport was originally named Windsor, but the name was changed to Stockport with the arrival of a Post Office in 1839 because there was already a Windsor Post Office elsewhere in Ohio.
2. Robert W. Naylor obituary, March 4, 1866, Local History and Genealogy Department, Washington County Public Library, Marietta, Ohio.
3. "An Ol' Time Volentine," u.d, Greg and Ellen Hill Collection of Naylor Material, Malta, Ohio.
4. James Ball Naylor, *Rambling Reminiscences*, Herald Printing Co., McConnelville, OH, 1927, 3.
5. Naylor, "Physicians of Morgan County," *Morgan County Herald*, February 4, 1926.
6. "A Remarkable Woman," *Logan Republican*, December 25, 1919.
7. Ruth Henery was either Naylor's mother's sister who also married a Henery or she became his mother's sister-in-law when his mother married John Henery.
8. Naylor, *Rambling Reminiscences*, 29.
9. The seven children were: Francis Wells, Harry Frederick, Warren L., Carlos Clyde, Samuel T., Mary Myrtle and Cleson R., Nancy Henery Obituary, April 1925.
10. James Ball Naylor, *The Kentuckian*, Boston: C.M. Clark Publishing Co., 1905, 10.
11. Naylor, *Rambling Reminiscences*, 17.

Notes

12. Naylor, *Rambling Reminiscences*, 5; Clancy, a close friend of Naylor, lived near Stockport and afterwards became a merchant in McConnelsville and later retired on a farm east of the river.
13. Ibid.; "Ague" is an old-fashioned term meaning a fever marked by paroxysms of chills, fever, and sweating that occur at regular intervals, as from malaria.
14. James Ball Naylor, "Physicians," February 4, 1926.
15. Ibid.
16. Naylor, *Rambling Reminiscences*, 11.
17. "Biographical Sketch of Dr. James Ball Naylor," *Tarboro's Book Review*, Tarboro, NC, June, 1901.
18. Naylor, *Rambling Reminiscences*, 11.
19. Naylor, "Two Men and a Boy," unpublished manuscript, Jean Naylor Finley Material.
20. Naylor, "Physicians," February 18, 1926.
21. Ibid.
22. Naylor, *Rambling Reminiscences*, 7.
23. Ibid.
24. Ibid., 35.
25. Ibid., 30.
26. Ibid., 36.
27. Naylor, "The Physicians," February 25, 1926.
28. "Biographical Sketch".
29. Naylor, *Rambling Reminiscences*, 16.
30. Naylor, *From Jim to Jack; Letters to an Old Time Schoolmate*, McConnellsville, Ohio: Herald Printing Co., 1907, 4.
31. "Biographical Sketch."
32. Norris F. Schneider, "Interviewing the Dean of Ohio Novelists," *Cleveland Plain Dealer*, November 3, 1935.

Chapter 2: What are you going to be?

33. James M. Rusk, "Reminescences and Etchings of S.Q. Lapius," April 21, 1894, Hill Collection.
34. James Ball Naylor, "Straight Sticks From the Brush of Old Morgan County," *The Weekly Herald*, July 20, 1939.
35. Naylor, *Rambling Reminiscences*, 23.
36. Roberta Swindell, "An Interview with Dr. Naylor," March 13, 1941, Hill Collection.
37. "Biographical Sketch."
38. Naylor, *Rambling Reminiscences*, 23.
39. Norris F. Schneider, "Wove Plots for His Fiction Tales," *The Sunday Times-Signal*, Zanesville, Ohio, January 27, 1935.
40. Naylor, "The Physicians," February 25, 1926.

Notes

41. Schneider, "Wove Plots."
42. Charles Robertson, *History of Morgan County*. Chicago, 1886, 283; Naylor reveals Gatewood's personality "by quoting verbatim what Gatewood has to say of himself in The Morgan County History;" "Physicians," February 11, 1926.
43. Robertson, *History of Morgan County*, 283.
44. Ibid, 284.
45. Naylor, "Physicians," February 25, 1926.
46. *The Morgan County Herald*, May 14, 1886; Swindell, "Interview with Naylor," Naylor." *The Morgan County Herald*, March 13, 1941.
47. *The Morgan County Herald*, McConnelsville, Ohio. May 14, 1886.
48. *New York Journal*, April 20, 1901, Scrapbook of Book Reviews, Finley Material, 7.
49. "Windsor Local Notes," *Morgan County Democrat*, June 24, 1887.
50. *The Morgan County Herald*, June 24, 1887.
51. *The Morgan County Herald*, July 20, 1888; Chester P. Swett, M.D. letter to Author, Lancaster, Ohio, July 17, 1977.
52. Lucile Naylor, "Mother," *The Morgan County Herald*, August 7, 1952.
53. Ibid."
54. Lucile Naylor, "Grandfather's Diary—1857," n.d.
55. Naylor, "Mother."
56. Lucile Naylor, "James Ball Naylor," *Columbus Dispatch*, October 26, 1952.
57. Naylor, "Away Back When," n.d., Hill Collection.
58. Naylor, "James Ball Naylor."
59. Naylor, "Away Back When."
60. Naylor, "Mother."
61. Naylor, "Away Back When."
62. D. W. Garber, Interview with Lucile Naylor, November 29, 1967.
63. "Biographical Sketch."

Chapter 3: S. Q. Lapius Emerges

64. Schneider, "Dean of Ohio Novelists."
65. "Morgan County's Poet," n.d., Book Reviews, 2.
66. "The Muskingum Valley. A Display of the Poetic Talent of Morgan County," August 24th, 1889, Hill Collection.
67. Rusk, "Reminiscences;" As recently as 1975, another physician, Dr. Charles Harris, appropriated the name and expanded it to Simon Quetin Lapius in his book *One Man's Medicine*, a factual journey of his training research and practice without acknowledgment of its prior use; Amazon.com, http://www.amazon.com/Mans-Medicine-Charles-Harris-M-D/dp/1412000165. (accessed October 27, 2008).
68. Schneider, "Wove Plots."

Notes

69. "A Sketch of Dr. J.B. Naylor, the Sweet Singer of the Muskingum Valley," 1896, Hill Collection.
70. Ibid.
71. "Among the Books," n.d., Book Reviews, 30.
72. Ibid.
73. "Current Coins," *The Daily Times Recorder*, Zanesville, Ohio, Book Reviews, 1 [1893].
74. Naylor, "Straight Sticks."
75. Rusk, "Reminescences."
76. Ibid.
77. *Cincinnati Commercial Gazette*, n.d., Book Reviews, 29.
78. Naylor, "A Peep into the Medical Future," *A Second Book of Vagrant Verse*, 1968, D. W. Garber, 2.
79. Garber and the author, interview of Schneider, Zanesville, Ohio, October 11, 1975.
80. Talent [Magazine], October, 1905.
81. Mildred Stephenson request from Victoria, Australia, April 10, 1903.
82. "Come Across with the Cash," n.d., Hill Collection.
83. "Buckwheat Bloom," "Frolic in the Firelight," "Like 'Er Ma," "The Ol' Fence Row," and "Pop-Paw Time" appeared in *Current Coins*.
84. Bruce Dye, A. A. Coulson's grandson, told the author that his grandfather paid for the printing of *Golden Rod and Thistle Down* and received one of the first books off the press, a single-digit, numbered copy of the two hundred printed.
85. "Biographical Sketch."
86. Naylor and his family were meticulous in maintaining scrapbooks of his works; however, unless the actual clipping included a date or place of publication, that information has been lost.
87. Naylor coined the name "Malconta," a combination of Malta and McConnelsville, still in evidence today as the name of American Legion Post 24.
88. Walker, "Stockport, Ohio: A Compendium"; The railroad held special memories for Naylor. He knew all of the conductors and engineers on the line. Ed Reynolds, a conductor on the Zanesville-Marietta run of the Baltimore and Ohio from 1881 to 1938, was one of his very dear friends. When Ed retired at the age of seventy-two, Naylor read "Ed Reynolds," a poem written just for the retirement ceremony.

Chapter 4: Pleasures and Passions

89. *The Columbus State Journal*, "In the Days of St. Clair", November 28, 1897, 4; Lena Ervilla, the fourth daughter, was named after her mother.
90. S. Q. Lapius, "Blue Eyes are Peeping at Me," *Golden Rod and Thistle Down*, Columbus, Ohio, Hann and Adair, Printers and Bookmakers, 1896, Verse 2, 56.

Notes

91. Lucile, "Mother."
92. Ibid.
93. The poem appears in *Golden Rod and Thistle Down, Songs From the Heart of Things*, and in *Book of Buckeye Verse*.
94. Effie Gregg, "A Tribute to James Ball Naylor," December 8, 1927, Finley Material.
95. Lucile Naylor and D.W. Garber interview, 6.
96. Lucile Naylor, "Mother."
97. Lucile Naylor, "Papa," October 4, 1951.
98. Ibid.
99. Naylor, "Mother."
100. Ben Hayes, "Dr. Naylor 'We may never see his like again,'" *Columbus Citizen*, April 8, 1945.
101. "Biographical Sketch."
102. Ibid.
103. James Ball Naylor, "Straight Sticks," August 3, 1939
104. Hayes, "We may never see."

Chapter 5: Serialized and Historical Fiction

105. Poynter on Line, "A Serial Narrative Primer," The Poynter Institute. http://www.poynter.org/column.asp?id-52&aid=56144, accessed May 5, 2010.
106. Wanda Mizer, "Pennsville Village Figured Prominently in Underground Railroad," August 23-29, 1979, *Chautauqua Souvenir Edition*, Morgan County, Ohio, 12.
107. Schneider, "Wove Plots."
108. "In the Days of St. Clair," *The Columbus State Journal*, November 28, 1897.
109. Ibid.
110. *The Ohio State Journal*, "Under Mad Anthony's Banner," November 6, 1898.
111. "Sign of the Prophet," *The Columbus state Journal*, Sunday, October 21, 1900.
112. Schneider, "Wove Plots."

Chapter 6: Success as a Novelist

113. Naylor, *Ralph Marlowe*, Akron, Ohio, 1901, Saalfield Publishing Co., 102.
114. "Ralph Marlowe," *New York Journal*, April 20, 1901, Book Reviews, 7.
115. Naylor, *Ralph Marlowe*, Preface.
116. Naylor, *From Jim to Jack*, 37.
117. Ibid., 38.
118. Ibid.
119. Ibid.
120. Akron Women's History, http://www3.uakron.edu/schlcomm/womenshistory/

Notes

saalfield_a.htm, (accessed January 5, 2010).
121. Naylor, *From Jim to Jack*, 34.
122. William Hilton, "The Printed Book," *Boston Home Journal*, May 18, 1901, Book Reviews, 5.
123. "Ralph Marlowe," *The Chronicle*, Newcastle England, July 4, 1901, Book Reviews, 9.
124. "Ralph Marlowe," *The Birmingham Daily Post*, Birmingham, England, July 5, 1901, Book Reviews, 34.
125. "A Yankee Yarn,", London, 1901, Book Reviews, 11.
126. "Ralph Marlowe," *New York Journal*.
127. "Ralph Marlowe," *Bookworm*, Birmingham, Alabama, April, 1901, Book Reviews, 32.
128. Naylor, *From Jim to Jack*, 34.
129. Ibid., 38
130. Ibid.
131. "Ralph Marlowe, Latest Ohio Novel," *Ohio State Journal*, January 13, 1901, Book Reviews, 33.
132. *Ralph Marlowe* and *In the Days of St. Clair* are known to have appeared with dust jackets as did, in all probability, the Saalfield editions of both *Under Mad Anthony's Banner* and *The Sign of the Prophet*.
133. Schneider, Notes of Interview with James Ball Naylor.
134. According to one of Naylor's cousins, a lady who was an avid collector of Naylor's books looked for "red books" at antique books stores, not realizing that all of his books also appeared with various distinctive covers.
135. Stephen J. May, Zane Grey. *Romancing the West*, Athens, Ohio: Ohio University Press, 1997.

Chapter 7: Marketable Endeavors

136. "The Ohio Magazine," *The Van Wert Daily Bulletin*, November 11, 1907.
137. The series *From Jim to Jack* was published as a pamphlet the following year (1907) by Herald Printing Company in McConnelsville, Ohio.
138. Schneider, "Morgan County Author, Who Died Last Week", *Zanesville Times Signal*, April 8, 1945.
139. Ibid.
140. Typewritten note signed by James Ball Naylor, Hill Collection.
141. Loretta Young, Letter to the author, October 27, 1976.
142. http://www.nhlibertycalendar.org/oldhome.php. This site lists contemporary dates and locations for Old Home Week celebrations.
143. Frank West Rollins, "How I Originated Old Home Week," *The Ladies' Home Journal*, August 1909.
144. Ibid.
145. Ibid.

Notes

146. VFM 1309 J.B. Naylor Papers, Letter from L. H. Bulkley, November 12, 1907: Ohio Historical Society.
147. VFM 1309 J.B. Naylor Papers, Letter to L. H. Bulkley, November 11, 1907: Ohio Historical Society.
148. VFM 1309 J.B. Naylor Papers, Letter to L. H. Bulkley, December 28, 1907: Ohio Historical Society.
149. VFM 1309 J.B. Naylor Papers, Letter to L. H. Bulkley, June 4, 1907: Ohio Historical Society.
150. Naylor, *Old Home Week*, Boston, The C.M. Clark Publishing Co., 1907, Foreward.
151. VFM 1309 J.B. Naylor, Papers, Letter to L.H. Bulkley, January 20, 1908: Ohio Historical Society.
152. "Songs From the Heart of Things," *The Ohio Magazine*, February, 1908.
153. D. J. McAdam, "Where the World Goes for Free Advice, 1997, http://www.djmcadam.com/flinch.html.
154. Naylor, "Angelina's Ardent Lovers," Finley Material.
155. Schneider, "Dean of Ohio Novelists."

Chapter 8: Writing for a Younger Audience

156. Jean Naylor Finley, Interview by the author, September 12, 1973.
157. Naylor, Diary entry, April 13, 1907.
158. Ibid., April 16, 1907.
159. *New York Sun*, November 3, 1906, Book Reviews, 40.
160. N.d., Book Reviews, 40.
161. *New York Times*, December 5, 1909, Book Reviews, 23.
162. *Columbus News*, December 12, 1909, Book Reviews, 44.
163. Naylor, *From Jim to Jack*, 3.
164. Naylor, *The Kentuckian*, C. M. Clark, Boston, Mass., 1905, Dedication.
165. *New York Times*, January 13, 1906. Book Reviews, 16.
166. Naylor, *The Kentuckian*, , 154.
167. Ibid., 155-156.
168 Naylor, *The Scalawags*, B. W. Dodge and Co., New York, 1907.
169. Naylor, Diary, March 18, 1907.
170. Finley Material.
171. The original handwritten manuscript of *Ralph Marlowe* shows very little sign of editing. Saalfield Collection, Kent State University Libraries.

Chapter 9: Speaker and Entertainer

172. A word coined by the Greeks taken from the "Temple of Apollo Lyceus," the walled garden where Aristotle taught.

Notes

173. "What Was Chautauqua," Chautauqua Souvenir Edition, *The Morgan County Herald*, August 23-29, 1976.
174. Harry P. Harrison, *Culture Under Canvas – The Story of Tent Chautauqua*, 1958, New York, NY, Hastings House Publishers, xvi.
175. Ibid., 52
176. The Redpath Collection at the University of Iowa contains a contract between Naylor and the Lyceum Bureau of Columbus, Ohio, that reveals previously unknown information about this aspect of Naylor's life.
177. Naylor, "The Circus," Life's Vaudeville, *The Daily Star*, May 8, 1915.
178. David Carlyon, "Wisconsin Circus Woes and the Great Dan Rice," *Wisconsin Magazine of History*, Summer 2005.
179. Naylor, "The Dan Rice Show," second stanza, *Songs From the Heart of Things*, New Franklin Printing Company, Columbus, Ohio, 1907, 137; *A Book of Buckeye Verse*, Tucker-Kenworthy Co., 1927, 14.
180. N.d., Book Reviews, 24.
181. Ibid., n.d., 46.
182. Lucile Naylor, "James Ball Naylor."
183. James Ball Naylor, "When You and I Were Boys," Program, 7.
184. N.d., Book Reviews, 24.
185. "Dr. Naylor and the Muskingum County Teachers' Institute," n.d., Finley Material.
186. "A Whole Evening of Rare Pleasure," n.d., Finley Material.
187. VFM 1309 J.B. Naylor Papers, Letter to L.H. Bulkley, 9 January 1908: Ohio Historical Society.
188. "Harrow Club Enjoys Evening with Naylor," *Ohio State Journal*, December 22, 1907.
189. Naylor, letter to Opha Moore, May 14, 1908.
190. Naylor, Diary, November 12, 1917.
191. It later appeared in a *Book of Buckeye Verse*, page 38.
192. "Guest in New York," n.d., Hill Collection.
193. "Dr. James Ball Naylor," *Caldwell Press*, April 20, 1904.
194. Naylor Contract with the Lyceum Bureau of Columbus, Ohio, May 1, 1905, Redpath Chautauqua Collection, Special Collections Department, University of Iowa Libraries, Iowa City, Iowa.
195. Ibid.
196. Ibid. The contract covers only the 1905-06 season.
197. Naylor, 1907 Naylor Diary, 15 entries.
198. Naylor, "James Ball Naylor In Heartfelt Poems and Homespun Yarns," n.d., Entertainment Program, Finley Material.
199. *The Tribune*, Toronto, Ohio, n.d., Book Reviews, 45
200. The poem, "Foolin' Ma" appeared as a broadside and was later published in in Naylor's *Vagrant Verse* in 1935.
201. "James Ball Naylor at Masonic Temple," n.d., Book Reviews, 24.

Notes

202. Woodsfield, Ohio, August 14, 1911.
203. "Rugged Individuals," n.d., *The Morgan County Herald*.
204. Editorial, n.d., *The Morgan County Herald*.
205. "Personal Glimpses, Olive Naylor Doty," n.d., Hill Collection.
206. Naylor, Diary, July 24, 1916.
207. "The Little Town of Toddville," *The Weekly Herald*, October 14, 1915.
208. "Zweistadt Players," *The Weekly Herald*, Octoaber 21, 1915.

Chapter 10: The Politician

209. Naylor, *Rambling Reminiscences*, 4.
210. Ibid., 30.
211. Ibid.
212. Naylor, "A Man and a Boy," Finley Material.
213. "'Doc' Mixes Muse with Politics," n.d., *Ohio Examiner*, Finley Material.
214. Hayes, Obituary.
215. "S. Q. Lapius Nominated," *Portsmouth Daily Times*, August 23, 1897.
216. Robert Wetherell, interview by the author, October 1975.
217. J. W. Tannehill to W. D. Matson, Editor and Publisher of *The Morgan County Herald*, *The Zanesville Times Signal*, April 12, 1945.
218. John W. Dean, *Warren G. Harding*, Time Books, Henry Holt and Company, New York, 2004, 25.
219. Naylor, "The Recent Feast of Unreason," McConnelsville, Ohio, November 14, 1910.
220. *The Marion Star*, June 23, 1910.
221. Tannehill to Matson.
222. State of Ohio, November 8, 1910 Election Results, Ninth-Fourteenth Senatorial District, 65.
223. "The Poet's Defeat," n.d., Finley Material.
224. Dorothy Barkhurst, "Dr. Naylor Finds Baseball Entertaining on Birthday," October 4, 1942.
225. N.d., Book Reviews, 53.
226. Ibid.
227. Naylor, "A Plea and a Promise", Malta Ohio, November 14, 1910.
228. Naylor, "The Recent Feast."
229. Ibid.
230. Ibid.
231. Ibid.
232. Ibid.
233. The name was changed to The National Republican Glee Club in 1992.
234. http://www.nationalrepublicangleeclub.org/History.htm, accessed April 9, 2010.
235. "Republican Campaign Songs for 1920," Columbus, Ohio, Republican State Executive Committee, 1921.

Notes

236. http://www.ohiohistorycentral.org/entry.php?rec=181, accessed April 5, 2010. Herrick was appointed Ambassador to France again in 1921 until his death in 1929; Naylor, Diary, January 29, 1916.
237. 1916.
238. "Rugged Individuals."
239. Naylor, Diary, August 11, 1920.
240. Ibid., August 30, 1920; A collection of these songs was published in 1920 by the Republican Glee Club and is a major rarity.
241. "'Ohio Star' Organ Republican Party," *Sandusky Star-Journal*, December 28, 1912.
242 Naylor, "The New Ohio Star," Sunshine Corner, *The Ohio Star*, January 4, 1913.
243. Naylor, "Forgets Washington," Life's Vaudeville, *The Marion Star*, February 4, 1916.
244. Naylor, "The New Secretary of State," Life's Vaudeville, *The Marion Star*, March 27, 1920.
245. Ibid.
246. Ibid.
247. Ibid.
248. http://www.findagrave.com/cgi-bin/fg.cgi?page=grGRid=10505367, accessed April 1, 2010.
249. David E. Dyvig, The National Prohibition Act, http://www.druglibrary.org/schaffer/library/studies/wick/wickla.html, eNotes.com, 2010.
250. Naylor, Diary, October 29, 1919.
251. Naylor, Life's Vaudeville, *The Marion Daily Star*.
252. Naylor, "Insidious Poison," *Ohio Star*, March 12, 1913.
253. Naylor, Life's Vaudeville, *The Marion Daily Star*.
254. Naylor, Life's Vaudeville, *The Marion Daily Star*.
255. Ibid.
256. Naylor, Life's Vaudeville, Marion Daily Star, May 4, 1915.
257. Naylor, "A Woman, A Wagon and A Horse," *Ohio Star*, March 15, 1913.
258. Naylor, *From Jim to Jack*, 51.
259. http://www.u-s-history.com/pages/h891.html.
260. http://history-world.org/wilson.htm, International World History Project. Accessed July 31, 2010.
261. Naylor, Diary, April 25, 1916.
262. http://millercenter.org/academic/americanpresident/wilson/essays/biography/5, accessed July 11, 2009.
263. Robert Naylor, letter to his parents, November 3, 1918.
264. Naylor, Diary.
265. Naylor, Diary, September 4, 1919.
266. "The Senate and the League of Nations," The United States Senate, http://www.senate.gov/reference/reference_item/Versailles.htm.

Notes

267. Naylor, Diary, November 20, 1919.
268. Naylor, "The Cosmopolite," Life's Vaudeville, *The Marion Star*, July 8, 1921.
269. Ibid.
270. Naylor, Diary, May 31, 1928.
271. Naylor, Diary, August 8, 1928.
272. Naylor, Diary, August 11, 1928.
273. Naylor, Diary, November 8, 1928.
274. Naylor, Diary
275. The average yearly income for all industries in 1920 was $1,407. http://usa.usembassy.de/etexts/his/e_prices1.htm, accessed on October 5, 2009.
276. Naylor, Diary, February 12, 1920.
277. *The Morgan County Herald*, McConnellsville, Ohio, December 8, 1955.
278. Naylor, Diary, June 12, 1920.
279. MIC 3 Warren G. Harding Papers [microform], Letter from George B. Christian, Jr. to J. E. Russell, August 30, 1921: Ohio Historical Society.
280. Newspaper article, May, 1921.
281. Naylor, Diary, August 3, 1923.
282. Naylor, Diary, September 26, 1923.
283. Eugene P. Trani, *The Presidency of Warren G. Harding.* 1977, The Regents Press of Kansas, 49; Naylor, Diary, June 13, 1924.
284. Naylor, Diary, August 16, 1924.
285. Naylor, Diary, August 23, 1924.
286. Naylor, "Scissors," Life's Vaudeville, The Marion *Daily Star*, September 4, 1923.
287. Naylor, Diary, September 8, 1924.

Chapter 11: The Last Years

288. Naylor, Dairy, October 19, 1926.
289. Naylor, Diary, October 23, 1926.
290. Naylor, Diary, November 2, 1926.
291. Hayes, "We may never see".
292. Naylor, Diary.
293. Naylor, *Rambling Reminiscences*, 7.
294. Naylor, Diary, Septrember 9, 1929.
295. Schneider, "Dr. Naylor of Malta Wrote Books," *Zanesville Times Signal*, June 16, 1940.
296. Dawes, handwritten inscription, *Book of Buckeye Verse,* November 22, 1927.
297. Schneider, notes of interview with Naylor.
298. Olive Naylor Doty, Letter to Robert Naylor, Venice, California, January 2, 1934.
299. Wendell Sether, "Cloudburst's Havoc Told," n.d., Hill Collection.
300. This information was relayed by Jean Naylor Finley "off the record" because

Notes

Lucile was still alive at the time and Jean knew that she would be very upset if she were to find out.

301. "Dr. Naylor Honored by Rotarians," *The Morgan County Herald*, McConnelsville, OH, August 31, 1935.
302. Schneider, "Who Died Last Week;" "Marietta College To Confer Degree Upon Dr. Naylor," October 14, 1937.
303. G. O. McConagle, Eulogy at Naylor's Funeral, April, 1945.
304. "Historical Novels," n.d., Hill Collection.
305. "Dr. Naylor Works in Public Library at Moscow," n.d., Finley Material.
306. "Ralph Marlowe," January 2, 1930.
307. Lucile Naylor, "James Ball Naylor."
308. Naylor, *The Sign of the Prophet,* Fredonia Books, Amsterdam, The Netherlands, 2002.
309. Publishers include Kessiner Publishing, INDY Publishers, Wildside Press.
310. http://www.kessinger.net/searchresults-orderthebook.php?Author=Naylor,+James+Ball. (July 15, 2009) The Fredonia Books reprinted *The Sign of the Prophet* in 2002. *The* Kentuckian, *The Sign of the Prophet, Goldenrod and Thistledown, Ralph Marlowe,* and *Misadventures of Marjory* have all been reprinted by Kessinger Publishers and other companies; *Under Mad Anthony's Banner, The Scalawags*, and *Old Home Week* have been reprinted more recently.
311. Mr. Frash, "In recognition of Dr. James Ball Naylor, Ohio physician, poet and novelist," Resolution, Ohio 96th General Assembly of the Ohio House of Representatives, April 18, 1945.
312. Charles Barrell, "To James Ball Naylor, Our Morgan County Poet," *The Morgan County Herald*, June 29, 1939.

Acknowledgments

Special thanks to the three most important people in my life: to my husband Gerry, who is always there for me, providing love, support, and anything else I might need or want; to my daughter Vicki for her thoughtful and insightful contributions to the manuscript during the final stage; and to my son Michael for his advice and help with the illustrations, photographs, layout, and cover design. The greatest measure of appreciation goes to my friend and mentor, D. W. Garber, for his enduring faith, encouragement, and generosity.

Additional credit is due to the kind and able assistance of librarians and individuals who contributed of their time in providing information and anecdotes that were essential for its completion. Among those to whom grateful acknowledgment is made for their help and encouragement during my trips to Ohio are Ms. Liz Plummer, Department Head, Reference Services, Ohio Historical Society; Ms. Blythe Shubert, Librarian, Kate Love Simpson Library, McConnelsville; Ms. Rebecca L. Cooley, Morgan County Recorder; Ms. Geraldine Reed and Ms. Betty White, Morgan County Historical Society Museum and Button House. Ms. Dottie Singer, in Stockport, was most helpful in finding a history of Stockport from Mr. and Mrs. Hank Faires, a delightful couple in their nineties. Ms. Brenda Casto provided genealogy information on the Naylor family. Mr. Dayle Selvus was a fount of knowledge about McConnelsville, and Mr. Bruce Dye provided additional information. Mr. Rick Shriver graciously provided digital copies

Acknowledgments

of area photos from original plates from the turn of the twentieth century. A special thank you goes to Ms. Sara Hurst, *Morgan County Herald*, who helped me in so many ways, from finding a great spot to park our motor home to searching for information in the newspapers archives, and especially for arranging a meeting with Greg and Ellen Hill who live in the restored "Elmhurst," Naylor's former home. Grateful acknowledgment is made to the Hills for their hospitality for I found some wonderful new nuggets of information in the material they so graciously allowed me to copy.

At Marietta College in Marietta, Ohio, Ms. Linda Showalter, Librarian, Special Collections, Marietta College, provided access to their collection of Naylor material. In Columbus, Ms. Barbara Meister, Librarian, Ohioana Library, provided access to the Pauline Gillespie collection that includes scrapbooks and correspondence with Lucile Naylor and various articles about Naylor. At the University of Iowa Libraries, Ms. Kathryn Hodson was especially helpful in searching the University's Redpath Chautauqua Collection.

A debt of gratitude goes to Dr. James Mason for educating me on the fine points of eBay bidding. With his help, a number of Naylor's books were added to my collection. In addition, his continuing interest and enthusiastic support of the project has been especially encouraging.

Much of the research was done more than thirty years ago. Among the number from that period to whom grateful acknowledgment is made are Doctor Naylor's daughters Lucile and Jean, his son Robert, and Robert's widow Edith. By making available their personal scrapbooks containing their father's writing and graciously loaning his diaries and personal memorabilia, a closer understanding of his personality and beliefs are possible.

Mr. Robert Wetherell, a venerable cousin of the Naylor family, served as a guide in visiting the site of the Naylor homestead where the author was born, the Baily and Newton ridge areas with their close association with Dr. Naylor's early years, the cemeteries where the family forebears are buried, and where old school houses were once located that were the scene of Naylor's boyhood activities and where he later taught.

Acknowledgments

Mr. Robert A. Tibbetts, Curator of Special Collections, and his assistant, Mrs. Helen Wada, at the Ohio State University Library, made available manuscripts and books from Dr. Naylor's library. And Mr. Thomas H. Hartig, Academic Librarian, and Mr. Conrad Weitzel, Reference Librarian, at the Ohio Historical Society were especially helpful. Mrs. Martha Townsend, Chief Reference Librarian, Santa Monica Library, made a diligent search and located the name and address of a contact that opened a broad field of research.

Mrs. Charlotte Harriss, Reference Librarian at the California State Library, Sacramento, provided advice and guidance, and Ms. Joy Mazza, Librarian, Kate Love Simpson Library, McConnelsville, both provided freedom of access to, and assistance in cataloging the library's excellent Naylor collection. Mr. Patrick J. Mullin, Special Collections Librarian, Dawes Memorial Library, Marietta; the Bancroft Library at the University of California, Berkeley; and the Henry E. Huntington Library, San Marino, were sources of information. The Library of Congress was also checked for Naylor material.

At McConnelsville thirty years ago, kind assistance was received from the following: Mrs. Martha Porter of *The Morgan County Herald*, Mrs. Helen Dugan, Mrs. Alice Hock, Ms. Maydell Alderman, and Mr. Charles Embree. Mrs. Harry J. Westerman, widow of the artist who was a longtime friend of the Naylor family, in interviews and correspondence provided interesting anecdotes, and her daughter, Mrs. Fred Redding, recalled her pleasant association with the Naylor children.

Mr. Norris Schneider, who published significant information about Dr. Naylor from personal interviews, generously made available his notes concerning his contacts and appraisal of the author and provided photographs from his collection.

Dr. Chester P. Swett of Lancaster, who wrote an article about Dr. Naylor for the *Journal of the Ohio Medical Society*, not only provided a copy of his article, but he drove to Malta to meet with Robert Naylor to clarify information previously obtained.

Miss Loretta Young provided information not available elsewhere. Mrs. Melanie McBride prepared a map of the local area from a map of Morgan County, and Mrs. Pat Jackson and Miss Cheryl O'Grady provided editorial assistance.

Acknowledgments

Mr. and Mrs. Robert A. Carter provided transportation and generous hospitality while time was spent searching for information in Ohio many years ago. It was a pleasure to renew our friendship again in the last few years.

To all of these, and to unnamed persons who gave unselfish assistance, sincere thanks are offered, for without their kindness and generosity much of interest concerning Dr. James Ball Naylor would have been lost.

Writings of James Ball Naylor

Collected Verse

1893	*Current Coins Picked Up at a Country Railway Station*, S. Q. Lapius, Columbus, Ohio, Hann & Adair, Printers and Bookmakers.
1896	*Golden Rod and Thistle Down*, S. Q. Lapius, Columbus, Ohio., Hann & Adair, Printers and Bookmakers.
1906	*Old Home Week*, C. M. Clark Publishing Co., Boston, Mass.
1906-1907	*Old Home Week*, C. M. Clark Publishing Co., Boston, Mass. Governor Rollins Version, (double copyright).
1906-1907	*Old Home Week*, C. M. Clark Publishing Co., Boston, Mass. Mayor Fitzgerald Version, (double copyright).
1907	*Songs From the Heart of Things*, New Franklin Printing Company, Columbus, Ohio.
1927	*A Book of Buckeye Verse*, Tucker-Kenworthy Co. Press, Chicago, Ill.
1935	*Vagrant Verse*, Morgan County Herald, McConnelsville, Ohio.
1968	A *Second Book of Vagrant Verse*, Preface by Lucile Naylor, D. W. Garber. (One copy only).

Serialized Writings

1896-1897	"Beggars Awheel," *Ohio Farmer*, December 3, 1896 to January 21, 1897.
1897-1898	"In the Days of St. Clair," *Ohio State Journal*, December 5, 1897, to February 27, 1898.
1898-1899	"Under Mad Anthony's Banner," *Ohio State Journal*, November 27, 1898, to March 5, 1899.
1900-1901	"The Sign of the Prophet," *Ohio State Journal*, October 28, 1900, to February 10, 1901.
1904	"The Witch Crow and Barney Bylow," *National Magazine*, V. 21, No. 3, December, 1904 through V. 22, No. 1, April, 1905.

Writings of James Ball Naylor

1905	"The Little Green Goblin of Goblinville," *National Magazine,* V. 22 and 23, September and October, 1905.
1906	"From Jim to Jack; Letters to an Old Time Schoolmate," *Ohio Magazine*, V. l, 1906.
1907-1908	"A Counterfeit Coin," *Ohio Magazine*, Columbus, Ohio, Vol. 3 and 4.
1926	"Physicians of Morgan County," *The Weekly Herald*, January 21, 1926 through March 4, 1926.
1927	"Rambling Reminiscences," *Morgan County Herald*, McConnelsville, Ohio, March 29, 1927.
1939	"Straight Sticks from the Brush of Old Morgan County," *Morgan County Herald*, McConnelsville, Ohio, June 15, 1939 through September 7, 1939.

Novels

1899	*Under Mad Anthony's Banner, Ohio State Journal,* Chauplin Press, Columbus, Ohio, 1899.
1901	*Ralph Marlowe*, Saalfield Publishing Co., Akron, Ohio.
1901	*The Sign of the Prophet*, Saalfield Publishing Co., Akron, Ohio.
1902	*In the Days of St. Clair*, Saalfield Publishing Co., Akron, Ohio.
1903	*Under Mad Anthony's Banner*, Saalfield Publishing Co., Akron, Ohio.
1904	*The Cabin in the Big Woods*, Saalfield Publishing Co., Akron, Ohio.
1905	The *Kentuckian*, C. M. Clark Publishing Co., Boston, Mass.
1907	*The Scalawags*, B. W. Dodge and Co., New York.
1908	The *Misadventures of Marjory*, C. M. Clark Publishing Co., Boston, Mass.

Children's Books

1906	*Witch Crow and Barney Bylow*, Saalfield Publishing Co., Akron, Ohio.
1907	*The Little Green Goblin*, Saalfield Publishing Co., Akron, Ohio.
1909	*Dicky Delightful in Rainbow Land*, Saalfield Publishing Co., Akron, Ohio.

Pamphlets

1907	*From Jim to Jack*, Herald Printing Co., McConnelsville, Ohio.
1911	*Across the Miles*, Rustcraft, Kansas City, Mo.
1911	*UCT Booklet*, United Commercial Travelers, Zanesville, Ohio.
1911	*Angelina's Ardent Lovers*, Advertising Poem.
1912	*For You*, Rustcraft, Kansas City, Mo.
1912	*If You Were Here*, Rustcraft Co., Kansas City, Mo.

Writings of James Ball Naylor

1912	*The Old Time Friend*, Rustcraft Co., Kansas City, Mo.
1921	*Old Morgan County*, Poem, Herald Printing Co., McConnelsville, Ohio.
1921	*The Muskingum Valley*, Malta, Ohio, June, 1919.
1927	*Rambling Reminiscences*, Herald Printing Co., McConnelsville, Ohio.
--	*Flinch*, Advertising Poem.

Short Stories

1897	"Ben's Adventure," S. Q. Lapius, Copyright 1897.
1903	"Ol' Cap Mingo," *National Magazine*, V. 17, No. 4, January, 1903.
1903	"How Tom Evans Won his Wife," *National Magazine*, V. 17, No. 5, February, 1903.
1903	"The Mishaps of Ol' Andy Perdue," *National Magazine*, V. 17, No. 6, March 1903.
1903	"A Lucky Opal," *National Magazine*, V. 18, No. 4, July, 1903.
1903	"Sim Spike's Misadventures," *National Magazine*, V. 19, October, 1903 (reference to)
1903	"The Youthful Indescretions of Jim Whiss," *National Magazine*, V. 19, October, 1903 Reference to *Ohio Star*, August, 1909.
1906	"The Undoing of Old John Chaney," *Ohio Magazine*, V. 4., 1906
--	"Coming of Sawlus," S. Q. Lapius.
--	"Did It Pay?," S. Q. Lapius.
--	"Jud Trainor's Ghost," *Ohio State Journal*.
--	"Mamie's Prisoner," *Ohio State Journal*.
--	"The Diversions of Dicky Dare."
--	"The Blackmer Affair," S. Q. Lapius.
--	"The Mills of the Gods," S. Q. Lapius.
--	"One of Morgan's Men," S. Q. Lapius
--	"Spike from the Underground Railway," S. Q. Lapius.
--	"Story of a Skeleton," S. Q. Lapius.
--	"Stuff of Which Doctors are Made," S. Q. Lapius.
--	"Two Consultations at Mam Sterlings," S. Q. Lapius.
--	"Wild Tom," S. Q. Lapius

Newspaper Columns

1913	*The Ohio Star*, Marion, Ohio.
1913	"Sunshine Corner," *The Marion Star*, Marion, Ohio.
1915-1923	"Life's Vaudeville," *The Marion Star*, Marion, Ohio.
1920-1923	*The Chicago Journal of Commerce*, Chicago, Illinois.
1925-1928	*The Week*.

Writings of James Ball Naylor

Political Sketches (Who's You in Ohio)

--	Allen Oh! Meyers
--	An'-drew Lightning Harris
1907	Charles Hungry Grosvenor
1907	Elmer C. Dover
1907	George Boss Cox
1907	Jon'ah McLean
1907	Joseph Beensome Foraker
1907	Kernel William Alexander Taylor
1907	May-Jar Charles Dick
--	Nickle-Us Longworth
1907	Theodore Energy Burton
1907	Tom Lofty Johnson
1907	William How-Hard Taft

Campaign Songs

1920	Republican Campaign Songs, Ohio Republican State Executive Committee, Columbus, Ohio.

Presented in Programs

1904	A Voice from the Past
1904	Down Upon the Rappahannock
1904	Flinch
1904	Follerin' the Fife and Drum
1904	My Skies are Seldom Gray
1904	The Fifer of the Buck Run Band
1904	The Girl Who Sings Popular Songs
1904	The Ol' Country Dance
1904	The Physical Culture Fad
1904	The Song in My Heart
1908	Foolin' Ma
1908	Song of the Motor Car
1908	The Cumberland Stage
1917	Old Glory, April 19, 1917
1917	Some Singers, June 4, 1917
1923	Minor American Singers, August 20, 1923
--	Boyhood Days
--	One Country, One People, One Flag
--	Pop Goes the Weasel
	Snip, A Study of a Boy and his Dog
	The Diversions of Dicky Dare
	The Jester

Writings of James Ball Naylor

The Millionaire Dude
When You and I Were Boys
Whistling Jimmy

Christmas Cards

Christmas in the Heart
From a Friend in Old Morgan County
Good Luck to You
Holiday Greetings
The Home Light
The Old Home Place

Broadsides

Bully Yankee
Call Him, Can Him and Cuss Him
Dr. John Goodfellow--Office Upstairs
Foolin' Ma
Gallery of the Immortals
Hands Across the Sea
My Laddie's Life Lesson
The One Flag
To Her Who Keeps My Dwelling Place
Ye Doctor's Life
Yours and Mine
What America Means

Unpublished Material

1908	Castle of Doors and Shutters, Children's story.
	The Fate of the Valley Belle, (A Barefoot Avenger), Story.
	Two Men and a Boy, Story.
	The Adventures of the Elephant, the Monkey and the Clown, Poem.
	The Cowboy and the Doctor, Comedy Sketch.
	Two of a Kind, Comedy Sketch.
1916	The Little Town of Toddville, Play.
	The Jackies, Play.
	One Country, Entertainment Program.
	When You and I Were Boys, Entertainment Program.

Bibliography

Accinelli, Robert D. "Was There a 'New' Harding? Warren G. Harding and the World Court Issue, 1920-1923." *Ohio History.* Vol. 84, Autumn 1975, No. 4. The Ohio Historical Society, 1975.

Allman, C. B. *Lewis Wetzel, Indian Fighter.* New York: Devin-Adair Company, 1961.

Binkley, Wilfred E. *American Political Parties.* New York: Alfred A. Knopf, 1958.

Brady, Cyrus Townsend. *A Doctor of Philosophy.* New York: Charles Scribner's & Sons, 1903.

Butterfield, Consul Willshire. *History of the Girtys.* Cincinnati: Robert Clarke and Co., 1890.

Cooper, James Fenimore. *The Deerslayer.* New York: Charles Scribner's & Sons, 1925.

Cooper, James Fenimore. *The Last of the Mohicans.* New York: Dodd, Mead & Company, 1951.

Coyle, William. *Ohio Authors and Their Books.* Cleveland, Ohio: The World Publishing Co., 1962.

De Hass, Wills. *History of the Early Settlement and Indian Wars of Western Virginia.* Wheeling: H. Hoblitzell, 1851.

Dean, John W. *Warren G. Harding,* New York, NY: Time Books, Henry Holt and Company, 2004.

Doddridge, Joseph. *Notes on the Settlement and Indian Wars.* Pittsburgh: J. S. Ritenour and W. T. Lindsey, 1912.

Faulkner, Harold U. *From Versailles to the New Deal.* New Haven: Yale University Press, 1950.

Finley, Harold M., and Jerry L. Martin, Ph. D., Gregory M. Miller, Ph.D., *Harold: The Gifted Small Town Boy.* June, 1992.

Forman, Jonathan, B.A., M.D., *Medical History of Franklin Co., Ohio,* Columbus, Ohio, 1967.

Galbreath, Charles Burleigh. *Daniel Decatur Emmett: Author of Dixie.* Columbus, Ohio, 1904.

Bibliography

Gamble, Jay Mack. *Steamboats on the Muskingum*. Staten Island, NY: the Steamship Historical Society of America, 1971.

Grant, Bruce, *American Forts—Yesterday and Today*. New York: E.P. Dutton and Co., Inc., 1965.

Grey, Zane, *Betty Zane*. New York: Grosset and Dunlap, 1903. (Charles Francis Press)

———, *The Spirit of the Border*. New York: Grosset and Dunlap, 1906. (A.L. Burt and Co. New York)

———, *The Last Trail*. New York: Grosset and Dunlap, 1909. (A.L. Burt and Co. New York)

Gruber, Frank, *Zane Grey*. Cleveland: World Publishers, 1970.

Gutgesell, Stephen. *Guide to Ohio Newspapers 1793-1973*. Columbus, Ohio: Ohio Historical Society, 1974.

Harrison, Harry P. *Culture Under Canvas – The Story of Tent Chautauqua*. New York, NY, Hastings House Publishers, 1958.

History of Southeastern Ohio and the Muskingum Valley, 1788-1928. Chicago, IL: Vol. III, The S.J. Clarke Publishing Co., 1928.

Howe, Henry. *Historical Collections of Ohio*. Cincinnati: Henry Howe, 1851.

Hulbert, Archer and David Butler. *Zeisberger's History of the Northern American Indians*. Ohio State Archaeological and Historical Society, 1905.

Humphries, Eck. *The Underground Railroad*. McConnelsville, Ohio: Herald Printing Company, 1931.

Jackson, Carlton, *Zane Grey*. Twayne Publishers, Inc. New York, 1973.

Kurland, Gerald. *Warren Harding, A President Betrayed by Friends*. SamHar Press, Charlotteville, NY, 1971.

Longworth, Alice Roosevelt, and Theodore Roosevelt, *The Desk Drawer Anthology*. Garden City, NJ: Doubleday, Doran & Company, Inc., 1937.

McKnight, Charles. *Our Western Border*. Philadephia, J.C. McCurdy & Co., 1876.

May, Stephen J., *Zane Grey. Romancing the West*. Athens, Ohio: Ohio University Press, 1997.

National Geographic. Vol. 153, No. 5, May 1978, 692.

Payne, Phillip G. *Dead Last, The Public Memory of Warren G. Harding's Scandalous Legacy*. Ohio: Ohio University Press, 2009.

Robertson, Charles. *History of Morgan County*. Chicago, IL, 1886.

Russell, Francis, *The Shadow of Blooming Grove: Warren G. Harding and his Times*. New York, NY: McGraw and Hill Publishing, 1968.

Schneider, Norris F. *Howard Chandler Christy*. Zanesville, Ohio, 1975.

———, *Zane Grey, The Man Whose Books Made the West Famous*. Zanesville, Ohio: by the author, 1967.

Snowden, James Ross. *The Cornplanter Memorial*. Harrisburg, PA: Singerly & Myers, 1867.

Springen, Donald. *William Jennings Bryan: Orator of Small-Town America*. Ann Arbor, MI: Greenwood Press, 1991. [Note: p 15]

Bibliography

Stille, Samuel Harden. *Ohio Builds a Nation*. Chicago, IL: The Arlendale Book House, 1939.

Trani, Eugene P., and Wilson, David L. *The Presidency of Warren G. Harding*. Lawrence, Kansas: The Regents Press of Kansas, 1977.

Walker, Richard, Ph. D. *Stockport, Ohio: A Compendium of Historical Information*. Sesquicentennial Committee, 1984.

Waterman, Nixon. *In Merry Mood*. Boston, MA: Forbes and Company, 1903.

Way, Frederick Way, Jr. *Way's Directory of Western Rivers' Packets*. By the author, 1950.

Online Sources:

Albert Edward Winship, http://en.wikipedia.org/wiki/Albert_Edward_Winship, (accessed March 3, 2009).

Bicycle History, http://www.marca.com/perico/eng/bicycle/history.html, (accessed March 4, 2008).

The Birth of Mass Media, http://www.well.com/art/maghist03.html, (accessed March 3, 2009).

Elihu Root, http://www.u-s-history.com/pages/h891.html, (accessed April 14, 2009).

Free Silver, http://www.micheloud.com/FXM/MH/Crime/index.htm, (accessed January 20, 2010).

Herbert Hoover, http://millercenter.org/academic/americanpresident/hoover/essays/biography/4, (accessed July 11, 2009).

Horatio Seymour, http://historical.ha.com/common/view_item.php?Sale_No=672&Lot_No=25292&src=pr, (accessed March 29, 2008).

Kirkwood College American Cultural History, http://kclibrary.nhmccd.edu/19[th]century1890.htm, (accessed November 5, 2009).

Underground Railroad, www.spartacus.schoolnet.co.uk/USASunderground.htm, (accessed November 15, 2009).

William Jennings Bryan's Cross of Gold Speech, http://historymatters.gmu.edu/d/5354.

Index

A

A Pleasant Journey, 115
Abbott, Kinney, 15
administration, 127, 135, 138-139,141
advertisement, 34
Aesculapius, 30
agent, 72, 138
agnostic, 48
Akron, Ohio, 62-63, 65, 67
America, 65, 91, 135-136, 140
American Jouranl of Education, 109
American Lyceum Association, 96
American Tobacco Company, 84
Americans, 56, 81, 129, 132, 135
analysis, 34, 52
anecdotes, 60, 147
announcement, 53, 55
appearance, 26, 32, 45, 52, 59, 67, 71, 75, 79, 91, 99, 104-105, 108-109, 133, 143
applause, 104, 113, 125
appointment, 127, 138
appreciation, 14, 63-64, 82, 104, 111, 113, 147-149
apprentice, 22, 48, 60
argument, 119, 137
article, 1-3, 55, 76, 104, 112, 121-123, 125-126, 129, 139, 142, 149
artist, 32-33, 84, 88, 167
artwork, 30, 81
aspirations, 21, 30, 90
attitude, 21, 38, 57, 71-72, 93, 114, 129, 134, 137, 139

audience, 58, 75, 85, 96, 99-104, 110-112, 115, 120, 125, 133
Australia, 34, 134
autobiographical, 72, 143
autograph, 13, 34-36

B

Babylon, 23, 59-61, 63, 72
Bald Eagle Creek, 8-9
Baltimore and Ohio railroad, 27
bankruptcy, 95, 144
barber, 34, 102, 119, 130, 142
Barwood, Dr., 61-62, 72
beard, 14, 23, 42, 45
beliefs, 21, 23, 31, 48, 114, 129, 166
Big Bottom, 54
biographic, 1-3, 30, 47, 61, 72, 142-143
birth, 5, 26
blood, 6, 34, 38, 74, 140
body, 28, 38, 51, 146
book, 8, 13, 19-20, 26, 30-31, 48, 52, 55, 57, 61-67, 70, 74, 76-82, 84, 86-89, 91,94-95, 100, 124, 131, 141, 143-145, 147, 150-151
bookings, 96,108-109
booklet, 72, 82-84, 142
Bookman's list of best sellers, 63
bookplate, 141
Boston Home Journal, 63
Boston, Massachusetts, 63-64, 76-78. 81, 95, 105, 108-109
boys, 9, 12-13, 17, 20, 32, 47, 50-51, 86-88, 90, 104, 114-115

Index

bride, 23, 52, 56
broadside, 72, 100
brochure, 109
Brooks, John, 60, 64
brother, 8, 12, 20, 24, 38, 56, 82, 86, 93, 106, 115, 144
Bryan, William Jennings, 118, 120
Bulkley, L. H., 80, 82, 105
bureaucratic, 137
Burnquist, J. A. A., 126
Burroughs Book Store, 66-67
Butler, Ohio, 1, 103
byline, 136
Bylow, Barney, 85, 87-88

C

Caldwell, Ohio, 104, 108
California, 115, 151
campaign, 10, 55, 81, 100, 112, 116-120, 123-126, 132, 138-139, 142,
campaign songs, 123, 125
Canada, 51, 78
candidate, 22, 117-124, 126, 128, 132, 134, 136
cane, 41, 147
career, 15, 29, 31, 70, 84, 92, 101, 104, 114-115, 120, 136, 151
Carleton, Will, 323
Carnegie, Andrew, 129
cartoonist, 52, 84
Century of Progress, 20
Chapple, Joe Mitchell, 73, 76
chapter, 50, 54, 63, 72, 87
character, 5, 21-23, 31-33, 37-39, 50, 54-55, 57-65, 68, 71, 72, 87-89, 91, 128, 149-150
characteristics, 89, 121
characterization, 37-38, 50, 68, 71-72, 88
Chatam, Vance, 90-91
Chautauqua, 75, 97-99, 112, 120, 139

Chesterhill, Ohio, 101
Chicago convention, 125
Chicago Journal of Commerce, 138-139
Chicago, Illinois, 20, 105, 115, 125, 144
children, 36-37, 40-41, 46-47, 49, 85-86, 94, 102, 108, 110, 114, 148
Children's Books
  Dickey Delightful in Rainbow Land, 87-88, 111;
  Little Green Goblin, 86-88;
  Witch Crow and Barney Bylow, 85, 87-88
Christy, Howard Chandler
  The Girl From Zanesville, 84
Cincinnati Commercial-Tribune, 81
circuit, 75, 96, 98-99, 109, 120
circumstances, 6, 20, 52, 57, 60, 71, 75, 86, 92, 103, 110
circus, 99-100, 130
Civil War, 5, 8, 10, 51-52, 116, 133
Clancy, Thomas D., 10, 15
Clovertown, 82
Collected Verse
  Book of Buckeye Verse, 144
  Current Coins Picked Up at a Country Railway Station, 30-31, 36, 40, 100, 143
  Golden Rod and Thistle Down, 36, 143
  Old Home Week, 77-79, 95, 105, 143
  Songs From the Heart of Things, 76, 80-83, 104-105, 143, 152
  Vagrant Verse, 147
collection, 1, 3-4, 30-32, 68, 142, 145, 147
college, 21-23, 92, 114, 147-148
Collier's Weekly, 129
Columbus Dispatch, 81
Columbus, Ohio, 2, 22, 25, 30, 36, 56, 68, 79, 81, 93, 105, 108, 124-126, 134
column, 125-126, 128-129, 131, 135, 138, 146
columnist, 125, 137

Index

commentaries, 100, 122
Company H, 6
comparisons, 57, 63, 122, 142
compliment 17, 32, 36
conductors, 51, 124
Confederate, 51
Congress, 117-118, 121, 128, 135-136, 138-139
consultation, 25, 37
contemporaries, 33, 53, 105, 111, 118, 151
contribution, 29-30, 53, 147, 151
controversy, 73, 93, 119, 135, 151
convention, 95, 125
convention, writers, 105
Cooke, Edmund Vance, 76, 81
Coolidge, Calvin, 20, 136, 138
Coshocton, Ohio, 109
Coulson building, 44
Coulson Store, 26, 44
Coulson, A. A., 26, 30, 36
country doctor, 3, 21, 24, 33, 75
cousin, 2, 9, 25-26, 30, 38, 55, 89, 97, 166
Cox, George, 122, 127
critic, 34, 53, 65, 67, 132
criticized, 86, 94, 119, 134
cronies, 34, 119

D

Dartmouth Medical College, 21
Daugherty, Harry, 125, 129, 140, 142
daughters, 1, 2, 26, 40, 86, 93, 108, 110-111, 114, 147
David Harum, 63
Dawes, Charles G., 20, 137, 139, 144
Dawes, Rufus R., 20, 143-144
Day, Holman, 111
death, 6, 11, 42, 139-140, 146-147, 150-151
dedicate, 77, 89, 106

Democrat, 100, 117-119, 127
Democrat, The, 29
Democratic, 118-121, 126-127
description, 30, 56, 59-60, 63, 88, 122
diagnostician, 28, 32, 136-137
dialect, 30, 33, 50, 57, 82, 100, 111
diary, 87, 92, 99, 109, 111, 114, 133, 139, 147
District Health Commissioner, 136-139, 143, 145
Doty, Charles H., 114
Doty, Weston, 114, 145
Doty, Winston, 114, 145
Doudna Run, 20, 46, 73
drama, 50, 73, 97, 102
druggist, 38
Duber Hamden Watch Factory, 149
Dunbar, Paul, 71

E

Eagleport, Ohio, 51
Edge, F. Gilbert, 79
edition, 30, 36, 55, 65-68, 79, 81, 95, 144, 151
editor, 31, 36, 53, 88, 106, 109, 112, 121, 125-128, 140, 143, 150
editorial, 107, 119, 125-126, 129-130, 136-138, 140, 142
education, 19-20, 96-97, 99
election, 26, 116, 119-128, 132, 136, 142
Elmhurst, 43-44, 47, 75, 115, 138, 149
engagement, 103-104, 133
entertainer, 34, 76, 96, 99, 101, 104-106, 108-109, 112, 114
entertainments, 34, 36, 100, 105, 108-109, 111
episode, 23, 37-38, 51-52, 54, 57, 59, 66, 68, 90
Eversull, Dr. H. K., 147
evidence, 38, 75, 130

Index

expenses, 20, 22, 74-75, 105, 109, 136
expression, 12, 14, 19, 100

F

fame, 4, 28, 66, 114, 141, 144, 147, 150, 152
fiction, 39-40, 50-53, 61
fictional, 51, 54, 56, 72, 91
fight, 6, 12, 21, 132-133, 137, 141
Finley, Raymond, 2, 7, 46, 48, 145
finances, 36, 63, 70, 73, 82, 94, 105, 108-109
Fire Fighters, The, 115
Fitzgerald, John F., 79
Flickinger, Samuel, 106
Flinch, 47, 83
Foraker, Joseph Benson, 122
France, 125, 132
friends, 13, 17-18, 20-21, 33-34, 36, 52, 73-75, 77-78, 82, 95, 104-106, 108, 111, 114, 119-120, 126, 139, 142-143, 147-148
fundamentalist, 14
funeral, 64, 75, 146

G

Garber, Dwight Wesley, 1, 23, 98, 103
Garber, J. S., 1, 98
Gatewood, Dr. Wesley Emmet, 21-23, 29, 48-49, 59, 62, 64
genius, 32-33, 110, 114, 132, 150
genre, 68, 87
Ghent, Belgium, 134
Gibson, Captain Charles J., 23, 62
Gibson, General John, 56
Gibson, Myrta, 23, 62
Girty, Simon, 55-56
goal, 20, 28
gold, 35, 118

Goodfellow, Dr. John, 73-76, 150
Grand Ole Opry, 77
grandmother, 6, 8, 11
grandparents, 115
grandsons, 115, 145, 148
Grey, Zane Pearl, 69
Grosvenor, Charles Henry, 122
Guest, Edward, 33

H

Hackney, Ohio, 112
Hagerstown, Maryland, 131
Hammond, Winfield, 126
Hann and Adair, 30, 36
hardback, 52, 55, 67-70, 87
Harding Club, 125
Harding, Warren Gamiel, 5, 119-121, 125-126, 133-142, 146
Harrow Club, 105-106
Hawkins, Fannie, 30
Heartfelt Poems and Homespun Yarns, 111
Henery, Alvanus, 14
Henery, John B., 8, 10
Henery, Ruth, 8, 16
hero, 56-58, 62, 71, 86, 116, 122
heroine, 56-58, 92, 94
Herrick, Myron T., 125, 133
high school, 20, 22
Hilton, William, 63
historic, 78
historical, 15, 50-53, 55, 57, 66-68, 70, 142, 151
historical novels, 52-53, 55, 68
history, 1, 52-54, 58, 68, 84, 118, 133, 138, 142, 157
Hooksburg, Ohio, 16
Hoover, Herbert, 136
House of Seven Gables, 79
Hubbard, Elbert, 132
Hughes, Charles Evan, 112, 132

Index

Hughes, Ruth, 13
humorist, 75, 96, 104
Humphrey, Dr. H., 139
Hunt, Colonel John Morgan, 51

I

ideas, 29, 82, 126, 128
identity, 38, 52, 57, 70, 91, 94
illustrations, 52, 78-79, 81-82, 122
imagination, 14, 22, 37, 39-40
inauguration, 138, 147
incidents, 13, 36, 51, 53, 60-61, 88, 143
income, 26, 70, 73, 95, 109, 144
Indians, 54-57
inscription, 75
inspiration, 9, 14, 29, 60, 68, 77, 82, 85, 99, 147
integrity, 148, 152
introductory, 80, 100, 125

K

Kean, Link, 73
Kennedy, President, 79
Kentucky, 56, 81
Kikertown, 51
kindness, 13, 20, 75
Kinney, Charles, 106
Kirkpatrick, William, 79

L

language, 32-33, 87-88
Lapius, S. Q., 29-30, 32, 70, 72, 100-101, 121
laughter, 12, 46, 104, 111, 146
leader, 56, 90-91, 119-120, 124-125, 127, 132, 136, 138-139, 146
League of Nations, 134-135, 140

lecturer, 104, 114
legislation, 123
legislative, 120, 123
letter, 13, 62, 72, 77, 89, 93, 131
letters, use of, 61, 89, 90
library, 19, 68
literary, 29-30, 62-63, 96, 125, 136, 147, 150-152
literature, 19-20, 31, 64, 112, 147, 151
locale, 31, 68, 77, 98, 100
Lodge Night, 115
London, England, 50, 64
Longworth, Nicholas, 122
lyceum, 96-99, 108-109

M

magazine, 70, 87, 100
majority, 135, 138
Malconta, 39
Malta, 1, 5-6, 8, 13, 15, 20, 26-28, 31, 37, 42-46, 68, 72, 75, 97, 114, 119, 121, 131-139, 142-143, 147-148
Manly, Aunt Lydia, 13
manner, 33, 45, 64, 71, 101, 122, 150
manuscript, 55, 62-63, 68, 71-73, 144
Marietta Academy, 20
Marietta College, 147-148
Marietta, Ohio, 5, 20, 55, 91, 137
Marion Star, 119, 125-126, 138-139
Marion Weekly Star, 125
Marion, Ohio, 125
marketable, 66, 70
Marlowe, Ralph (the character), 59-63, 89
marriage, 8, 24, 38, 52, 84, 93, 114
Masonic, 111, 135
Massachusetts, 35, 78
Matson, W. D., 143
McConnelsville, Ohio, 2, 5, 10-11, 16, 29-31, 43, 51, 75, 97, 115, 118, 123, 139, 147

Index

McDermott, John, 20
measles, 11
medical practice, 21, 24-28, 37, 40, 58 136, 148
meetings, 14, 58, 97, 104-107, 109, 125, 130, 137, 139, 157
mentor, 18, 32, 61, 91
Methodist, 14, 19, 26, 49
mills, 9, 51
miners, 128, 134
misinterpret, 61, 89
Mission Ridge, battle of, 6
money, 13, 16, 20-21, 26, 30, 36, 62, 67, 71, 113, 122, 133
Moore, Opha, 106
Morgan County, 5, 20, 27-28, 30, 32, 51, 54, 80, 100, 104, 117, 120-121, 123, 136-138, 142, 153
Morgan County Herald, 42-43, 97, 131, 142, 147, 152
Morgan County Historical Society, ii, 25, 79
Morgan, General John Hunt, 51
Moscow, Russia, 149-150
movies, 96, 99, 115
music, 30, 97, 102, 110-111, 124, 146
Muskingum Count Medical Society, 102
Muskingum River, 5, 14, 31, 35, 51, 54
Muskingum Valley, 5, 14, 29, 42, 69, 91, 151
Muskingum Valley Chautauqua, 97
mystery, 38, 61, 71, 84

N

narrative, 55, 57, 72, 88-89
National Geographic Magazine, 76
National Magazine, 71, 73, 76, 85-86
National Prohibition Act, 128
Naylor's office, 27, 30, 37-38, 40, 44
Naylor, Abigail (Ball), 6

Naylor, Annie Budee, 40, 48, 85, 93, 110, 149
Naylor, Bonnie Jean, 2, 44, 48, 85-87, 93, 110, 115, 146, 147
Naylor, James Ball, 1-2, 5, 10, 68, 73, 85, 102, 105-106, 135, 141, 146
  as a boy, 5-17, 40-51
  finances, 36, 63, 70, 73, 82, 94, 105, 108-109
  relationship with Gatewood, 21-22, 29, 48, 62
  relationship with Rusk, 32, 90
Naylor, James Robert (son), 42, 44, 46-48, 68, 85, 88-89, 93, 110-111, 134, 138, 147, 149
Naylor, John Thompson Leslie, 24
Naylor, Lena Ervilla (daughter), 40, 48, 85, 93, 110-111, 149
Naylor, Lena Ervilla (Naylor), 24-26, 30, 36-37, 40-41, 43, 45-46, 48-49, 71, 146
Naylor, Nancy (Wells), 6
Naylor, Nettie Lucile, 1-2, 27, 40-41, 44, 47-48, 85, 93, 106, 108-109, 111, 148-150
Naylor, Olevia Ellen (Coulson), 25
Naylor, Olive Nance, 26, 40, 44, 48, 85, 92-93, 108-109, 111, 114-115, 142, 145-146, 149
Naylor, Robert W., 6
Naylor, Samuel, 6
neutrality, 131-132
New York, 64, 84, 87, 90, 95, 97, 105, 108, 116, 131, 134
news, 36, 131, 142
newspaper, 2, 23, 29-31, 37, 50, 52, 54, 63-64, 73, 75, 81, 100-101, 104, 119, 121, 123, 125-126, 141, 143, 149,151
Newspaper Columns
  Life's Vaudeville, 124, 135
  Sunshine Corner, 124
newspaperman, 2
Newton Ridge, 5, 8, 13-14, 23, 31

Index

Newton Ridge school, 15
1933 World's Fair, 19
nomination, 118, 123, 129, 132
novel, 1, 19, 34-36, 52-55, 58-59, 62-63, 66-67, 70, 77, 88-92, 95, 106, 112, 148, 151
Novelist, 34, 59, 112
Novels
  Cabin In the Big Woods, 1, 87
  In the Days of St. Clair, 53-54, 56-58, 66-67
  Kentuckian, The, 77, 89-91, 95, 149
  Misadventures of Marjory, The, 93-95
  Ralph Marlowe, 59-60, 61, 63-66, 68, 70, 72, 89, 91, 150
  Scalawags, The, 89, 91, 95
  Sign of the Prophet, The, 56-59, 66, 151
  Under Mad Anthony's Banner, 55-56, 58, 67
novels, 1, 19, 36, 52-55, 58, 66-68, 70, 79, 88-90, 93, 95, 106, 149, 151

O

obstetrical, 25
Ohio, 1-3, 5, 32, 40, 50, 54, 56, 63, 65, 79, 81-82, 89, 100-105, 108, 118, 120, 125, 127, 137, 150-152
Ohio Library Company, 79, 81-82, 105
Ohio Magazine, 71-72, 82
Ohio politics, 119, 132
Ohio State Senate, 118-120, 140
Ohio Society of New York, 108
Ohio State Journal, 50, 52-53, 56, 59, 66-68, 84, 122, 127
Ohio State Medical Board, 138
Ohio Volunteer Infantry, 6
One Terrible Day, 115
opal, 71
opinions, 62, 125-126, 151-152
opponent, 102, 120-121

opportunity, 9, 16, 39, 50, 57, 76, 105
orator, 96, 104, 118, 138
oratory, 97, 118, 124-125, 139, 135
Our Gang, 115

P

pamphlet, 53, 73, 84, 102, 147
Pamphlets
  Angelina's Ardent Lovers, 84
  From Jim to Jack, 72, 77, 103, 143
  Rambling Reminsicences, 143
patients, 25-29, 37, 44-45, 54, 58, 122, 137
patriotic, 44, 103, 132-133
Patterson, A. J., 84
Penn township, 6, 8
Pennsville, 24-26, 51, 54
performance, 104, 110
performed, 99, 110, 115, 137
performer, 98-99, 108
personality, 23, 38, 64, 71-72, 91, 110
Peter Pan, 115
photographer, 47, 125
photographs, 2, 66, 81, 100, 109
physician, 22-23, 26, 28, 37-39, 60, 142, 152
Physicians of Morgan County, 142
platform, 9, 70, 96-97, 99, 105, 109, 112, 124-125
Plays
  Little Town of Toddville, 115
Poems
  Cuba Libre, 134
  Down at Hughes Ol' Shop, 103
  Dr. John Goodfellow-Office Upstairs, 73-77, 150
  Follerin' the Fife An' Drum, 134
  Foolin' Ma, 111
  Gray Old Sauter Mill, 9
  Hide-an-Seek, 30
  In That Ol' Tobacker Patch, 30

Index

Jest Lazin' Round, 30
Jester, The, 112
Laddie Abiding With Me, The, 89
Like 'Er Ma, 30
Little Old Druggist, The, 30
Little White School House, The, 32
Millionaire Dude, The, 134
Muskingum Valley, The, 30, 73
My Skies are Seldom Grey, 112
My Time O' Year, 30
Newton Ridge (poem), 103
Ol' Fence Row, The, 30
Old Country Dance, The, 103
Old Morgan County, 73
Peep Into the Medical Future, A, 33
Pixy Band, The, 41
Pop-Paw Time, 30
Razzer Jim, 134
Typical Yankee Boy, 134
What's the Use, 141
poetry, 4, 14, 30, 33-34, 36, 40, 50, 53, 79, 82, 84, 95, 99-102, 111-112, 121, 142, 144
political, 11, 99-100, 116-117, 120-122, 124, 126, 129, 132, 136-137, 139, 142
politicians, 96, 116, 121, 127, 139
politics, 27, 40, 102, 108, 116, 119, 121-123, 125-127, 132, 136, 139, 142
popularity, 1, 3, 63, 66-67, 69, 97, 99, 108
presentations, 1, 102
principles, 126, 152
printing, 31, 37, 65, 105
production, 16, 65, 82, 94, 99, 101, 115
profession, 22, 28, 33, 37, 72
programs, 49, 96, 98, 99, 101-102, 110-112
Progressive, 126-127, 131
Prohibition, 121, 123, 128, 138
pseudonym, 30, 70, 91, 121
publication, 2, 30, 36, 52, 54, 63, 67, 70-72, 78-79, 88, 111, 125, 129
publisher, 3, 62, 66, 68, 77, 79, 82, 94-95, 105, 143-144, 151
publishing, 50, 62-63, 66, 82, 151
pulpit, 14, 96
pupil, 16-19, 91, 144

Q

Quaker, 6, 51, 101, 114-115

R

rabies, 143, 146
railway, 31
Randall, E. O., 106
reader, 37-38, 50-51, 56, 58, 61, 67, 72, 87, 89, 91
readings, 100-101, 111-112
recite, 17, 73, 75, 99, 101, 108, 111, 125
recognition, 17, 29, 70, 151
Redpath Lyceum Bureau, 98
reprinted, 121, 151
Republican, 10, 106, 116-117, 119, 123-125, 127, 131, 133-136, 138-139
reputation, 36, 105, 115, 118, 131-132, 134-136, 142
reviewers, 52, 63-65, 68
reviews, 31-32, 36, 66, 81-82, 87-88, 101, 110, 112
Rice, Dan, 99-100
Riley, James Whitcomb, 33, 111
role as a physician, 4, 152
Rollins, Governor Frank W., 77-78
Roosevelt, Theodore, 122, 126-127, 131-132, 134
Root, Elihu, 131
rotarians, 147
Rotary, Roses 147
royalties, 63, 95
Rusk, James M., 18-20, 23, 32-33, 90-91
Rust Craft, 82

Index

S

Saalfield Publishing Company, 62-63, 65-67, 87, 89, 95
Saalfield, Ada Louise Sutton, 63
Saalfield, Arthur J., 63
sarcasm, 22, 120, 152
satire, 128
scandal, 140
scene, 29, 39, 54, 77-78, 102, 114-115
scenery, 31, 47, 54
Schneider, Norris B., 60
Schneider, Norris, 2, 27, 143
school, 16-17, 19-20, 89-92, 97
script, 76, 103, 114
Secretary of Commerce, 136
Secretary of State, 127-128, 131
Secretary of the Interior, 140
Secretary of the Territory, 56
Secretary to the President, 138
Senate, United States, 126, 134-135, 139
Senate, Ohio State, 118-120, 140
senator, 121, 129, 132, 136
serialization, 53, 55-56, 67-68, 72, 87
serialized, 50, 52, 68
series, 71-73, 100, 115, 121-122, 142-143, 151
17th Regiment, 6
Seymour, Horatio, 116
Short Stories
  Beggars Awheel, 50
  Ben's Adventure, 51
  Blackmer Affair, The, 38, 94
  Coming of Sawlus, The, 38
  Counterfeit Coin, A, 72
  Diversions of Dicky Dare, The, 17, 111
  Jud Trainor's Ghost, 52
  Lucky Opal, A, 71
  One of Morgan's Men, 51, 91
  Spike from the Underground Rail Road, A, 51
  Stuff of Which Doctors are Made, 39, 91
  Two Consultations at Mam Sterlings, 37
  Undoing of Old John Chaney, 71
  Wild Tom, 39
short stories, 17, 36-37, 39, 52, 70-71, 89, 91, 94, 111
sister, 24-25, 44, 87
slavery, 6, 91
Socialist, 121, 127
society, 130-131
son, 2, 42, 68, 88, 134, 138, 147
southern, 51-52, 56
speaker (Naylor), 94, 99, 104, 112
speakers (others), 96, 110, 119-120, 125
speech, 44, 118, 120, 133-134
Starling Medical College, 22-23
steamboats, 5, 14-15
stepfather, 8-10, 14, 16, 19, 21, 116-117
Stockport Mill, 10
Stockport, Ohio, 5-6, 9-12, 14-16, 19-24, 54, 59-62, 115
success, 59-60, 63, 65-66, 73, 79, 82, 84, 90-91, 95, 101, 109

T

Taft, William Howard, 126
talent, 18, 70, 87, 99, 114, 151
Tales of Kentuck, 63
Teapot Dome, 140
testimonials, 81, 101, 108
theater, 92, 97, 114
threshing, 51
tobacco, 15, 62
Toronto, Ohio, 110
trilogy, 51, 54-55, 57, 64-66, 68
troupe, 108, 111
tuberculosis, 22
tutor, 19, 141

Index

Twain, Mark, 94, 109, 110
Twentieth century, 35, 39
twins, 24, 112-113, 142-144

U

Underground Railroad, 51
Union cause, 6

V

Valentine, 6
Vawter, Keith, 98
versifier, 34
volume, 31-33, 36, 65, 72, 76, 79-81, 100, 143
voters, 10, 116-117, 127

W

Waterman, Nixon, 81
Week, The, 142
Werner Company, 63, 65, 67
Westcott, Edward, 63
Westerman, Harry J., 52-53, 84, 106, 122
White, Dr. James W., 11-12
White, Howard, 118
Willis, Frank B., 127, 133
Wilson, Colonel, 106
Wilson, Woodrow, 113, 126-128, 131-132, 134-135
Windsor township, 8, 16
Winship, Dr. A. E., 81, 110
Wood, Dr., 13

Z

Zanesville, 2, 5, 15, 26, 32, 60, 68, 84, 92, 104, 112
Zanesville Signal, 140
Zanesville Times-Recorder, 32
Zanesville Times Signal, 140, 143
Zanesville United Commercial Travelers, 84
Zweistadt Players, 115

www.ingramcontent.com/pod-product-compliance
Ingram Content Group UK Ltd.
Pitfield, Milton Keynes, MK11 3LW, UK
UKHW040003250426
12049UKWH00032B/176/J